Instant Pot Air Fryer Crisp Cookbook for Beginners

Affordable, Easy and Delicious Recipes for Smart People on a Budget (21-Day Meal Plan)

Jarson Scoter

Table of contents

Chapter 1: Understanding the Instant Pot Duo Crisp

If you ever used to think that your Instant Pot pressure cooker does not provide all the cooking functions that you might need to prepare different sorts of meals, then here it is! Instant Pot has launched a 10 in one multipurpose kitchen appliance when it is no less than a technological marvel among all the home appliances. The Instant Pot Duo Crisp brings all the necessary cooking functions in a single vessel. Now whether you want to bake, Air fry, pressure cook, slow cook, sauté, dehydrate, broil, or roast your food, you can do it all in this single pot. With the changing lid function, Instant pot has brought great technology at your fingertips. The text this cookbook acknowledges the mastery of Instant Pot and promises to unfold the mysteries behind its basic functioning. We shall understand how to use this super-efficient cooking appliance up to its best use. And with that information, we will also try to make some of the delicious recipes in the new Instant Pot Duo Crisp.

The Benefits of Using Instant Pot Duo Crisp

The Instant Pot Duo Crisp is a convertible cooking appliance, and with a switch of a lid, the device can be converted into an Air fryer from a pressure cooker. And that's not just it; there are several other functions that you can use within this device.

1. One-Pot Cooking

The good news is that the basic design of the new Duo crisp air fryer is almost the same as the Instant Pot original series. So, it brought the same one-pot cooking formula into play, and now instead of the switch from pot to another, you can continue cooking a single meal using different cooking options. For an instant, if you want to first pressure cook the food, then broil then. You can do it just by replacing the lid on the top and selecting the desired method.

2. Ten Functions in One:

When you look at the control panel of this Instant Pot Air fryer, there are far many options than any other ordinary fryer. A total of ten cooking modes are given in the Duo crisp. The basic Instant pot functions along with the additional modes of Bake, Air fry, broil and dehydrate.

3. Energy and Time Efficient:

Instant Pot Duo Crisp barely takes a few minutes to get everything done. It is both time and energy-efficient. Once the food is cooked, the appliance switches to this "keep warm" mode, and minimum heat are used to keep the food fresh.

4. Changing Lids:

Forget about the days when you used to switch between different appliances. The best feature of this appliance is that it is so simple and easy to convert it from one form to another. There are two different lids that can be used to carry out a range of different functions. The pressure-cooking lid is used for pressure cooking modes, and with Air frying lid, you can bake, air fry and roast, etc.

5. User-Friendly:

Since the design is the same and as simple as the original Instant Pot pressure cooker series, the user wouldn't find much difficulty in understanding its control panel and its use. All button is labeled with their respective functions and the LED screen guides about the on-going operations.

Structure of the Instant Pot Duo Crisp

The basic build of the Instant Pot Duo Crisp is simple, but it is the different lids that need much of the understanding. When you unbox an Instant pot Duo Crisp, you shall find the following basic components and accessories.

- The base unit
- Air fryer lid
- Pressure cooking lid
- Inner pot
- Multi-functional Rack
- Broil or dehydrating tray
- Air Fry Basket base
- Multi-level Air fryer basket
- Storage cover
- User Manual

Unit Specifications

The entire unit of the Instant Pot Duo crisp can be discussed in two parts, the base unit, which carries the heating element at the bottom, the control panel on the outside and condensation collection, then there are these lids. The Specification of this unit are as follows:

- Power: 1500W
- Power Supply: 120V-60Hz
- Weight: 10.3Kg/22.7lb
- Dimensions (With air fryer lid): 14.76 in × 13.58 in × 15.28 in
- Dimensions: (With pressure cooker lid): 14.76 in × 13.58 in × 14.17 in

The Control Panel

The control panel of this appliance is present at the front of the base unit and carries two different types of keys: the functional and the operational keys. The operational keys give you the option to choose the desired smart program. The top series of the operational keys consist of:

1. Pressure Cook
2. Sauté
3. Slow Cook
4. Steam
5. Sous Vide.

These are all the smart operations which are operated using the pressure-cooking lid. The second series of smart programs are:

1. Air fry
2. Roast
3. Bake
4. Broil
5. Dehydrate

On either side of the LED screen, there are keys for Temp and Time. Using these keys, you can either increase or decrease the time and temperature. Then there are keys like: Keep warm, Start Cancel, and Delay start at the bottom of the control panel.

The Cooking Lids

Pressure Cooking Lid:

The pressure-cooking lid works like the basic Instant pot lid, which has a pressure valve which can be Closed or Opened to using its "Pressure release Handle." There is this float valve which is pressed to maintain the pressure inside when needed. The has a hand on top to easily remove it or to fix it on top of the base unit. You can use this lid to carry out the following functions.

1. Pressure Cook
2. Sauté
3. Slow Cook
4. Steam
5. Sous Vide

Air Fryer Lid:

The Air fryer lid appears different in structure than the pressure-cooking lid, and it consists of an air vent and a heating element on the inside. There is no valve control on this lid. It is simply placed on top of the base and rotated until it is sealed. You can use this lid to carry out the following functions:

1. Air Fry
2. Roast
3. Bake
4. Broil
5. Dehydrate

Inside the Base Unit

In order to cook different types of meals in different styles, the Instant pot Duo crisp comes with a range of removable components. Here are the components you can find inside the base unit.

1. The Multi-Layer Air fryer basket: It is used for air frying purposes, and you can also place it to roast or broil your food. The basket is multilayer, so you can adjust them as per your serving size.

2. Wire Rack: This multipurpose wire rack can be used for another function. To place a baking pan inside, or to place food directly on it.
3. Cooking pot: the cooking is pot is a place to sauté, pressure cook for slow cook the food inside the cooker.
4. Broil/Hydrating tray: this tray is placed at the bottom to dehydrate or broil the food.

Chapter 2: How to Use the Instant Pot Duo Crisp Air Fryer?

Now that we know all about the different parts of the Instant Pot Duo crisp, its about time to put this device to use. To carry out each smart program on this device, you would need to follow some simple steps.

Prepare the Device

- Begin by checking all its components and see if the power cord is intact and in good shape.
- Clean the device from inside and out using a cloth. And wash the removable pots or baskets if you are using it for the first time.
- Now plug in the device, and its LED Screen will automatically light indicating that it is ON.

How to Cook

1. To begin with, first, select the suitable accessories that are required to cook the meal. if you want to Air fry, the food then places the Air fryer base pan at the bottom of the Instant Pot.
2. If you want to simply pressure cook or slow cook etc. then insert the cooking pot in the Instant Pot. Similarly, you can also fix the wire rack to suit your needs.
3. After placing the pots or baskets in place, add the food to the Instant Pot.
4. If it is just sautéing, then simply press the Sauté button, and hit the start button, and the food will start sautéing.
5. To pressure cook food, put the Pressure-cooking lid and close the pressure valve then seal the lid. Press the Pressure Cook button and select time and temperature as desired. At the end of this program, you can either release the steam by turning the Pressure release handle or leave the appliance to naturally release the steam. Finally, remove its lid. This mechanism is applied for steaming.
6. Functions in which pressure cooking is not required, like Slow cooking, you can keep the pressure valve open after putting on the lid.
7. To cook using the Air fryer lid, after placing the food inside, simply put on the air fryer lid and rotate to seal it.

8. Choose bake, broil, roast, dehydrate or Air fry and select the time. The temperature for each operation is preset, which can be adjusted if needed.
9. You need to press Start after selecting both mode and its settings. After preheating, the appliance will automatically start the timer.
10. At the end of each program, the device beeps, and it switches to Keep Warm mode.
11. The cancel key is pressed to cancel any operation, including the Keep warm function.
12. Enjoy your delicious meal.

Cleaning and Maintenance

The Instant Pot Duo Crisp has this smart design which makes the cleaning extremely easy and convenient:

1. Allow your device to cool down at room temperature and unplug before any use.
2. Remove all its trays, pot, or basket and wash them in the dishwasher or wash using soap water. The washed components must be dried after washing.
3. Never wash both the pressure cooking and Air fryer lid; to clean them using a damp cloth and wipe them from the top. And gently clean from the inside using a cloth.
4. The Pressure handle of the pressure-cooking lid is removable so it can also remove and clean it.
5. Similarly avoid immersing the base unit water, instead use a damp cloth to wipe off its interior and exterior.
6. Put all the components back to their positions and use the device in the next cooking session.

Chapter 3: Breakfast Recipes

Sweet Potato Hash

Prep Time: 10 minutes
Cooking Time: 16 minutes
Serving: 4

Ingredients:

- 2 large sweet potato, cubed
- 2 slices bacon, cubed
- 2 tablespoons olive oil
- 1 tablespoon smoked paprika
- 1 teaspoon of sea salt
- 1 teaspoon ground black pepper
- 1 teaspoon dried dill weed

Method:

1. Toss sweet potato with bacon, salt, black pepper, olive oil, paprika, and dill in a large bowl.
2. Spread this sweet potato mixture in the Air Fryer Basket.
3. Set the Air Fryer Basket in the Instant Pot Duo.
4. Put on the Air Fryer lid and seal it.
5. Hit the "Air fry Button" and select 16 minutes of cooking time, then press "Start."
6. Toss the potatoes after 8 minutes then resume cooking.
7. Once the Instant Pot Duo beeps, remove its lid.
8. Serve.

Nutritional Information per Serving:

- Calories 200
- Total Fat 11.4g
- Saturated Fat 2.4g
- Cholesterol 10mg
- Sodium 721mg
- Total Carbohydrate 20.2g
- Dietary Fiber 3.8g
- Total Sugars 6g
- Protein 5.7g

Vegetable Hash

Prep Time: 10 minutes
Cooking Time: 29 minutes
Serving: 4

Ingredients:

- 1 1/2 lbs. potatoes, peeled and diced
- 1 tablespoon olive oil
- 1 red bell pepper, seeded and cubed
- 1 small onion, cubed
- 1 jalapeno, seeded and cubed
- 1/2 teaspoon olive oil
- 1/2 teaspoon taco seasoning
- 1/2 teaspoon ground cumin
- 1 pinch salt
- Ground black pepper to taste

Method:

1. Add potatoes to a bowl full of water and soak them for 20 minutes, then drain.
2. Dry the potatoes with a clean towel then toss them with ½ tablespoon olive oil in a bowl.
3. Spread the potatoes in the Air Fryer Basket.
4. Set the Air Fryer Basket in the Instant Pot Duo.
5. Put on the Air Fryer lid and seal it.
6. Hit the "Air fry Button" and select 18 minutes of cooking time, then press "Start."
7. Meanwhile, add bell pepper, jalapeno, and onion to the same bowl.
8. Stir in remaining olive oil, taco seasoning, salt, black pepper, and cumin.
9. Toss the veggies with the seasonings to coat them well.
10. Once the Instant Pot Duo beeps, remove its lid.
11. Transfer the potato to the vegetable bowl and toss well.
12. Return this mixture to the Air Fryer Basket.
13. Set the Air Fryer Basket in the Instant Pot Duo.
14. Put on the Air Fryer lid and seal it.
15. Hit the "Air fry Button" and select 11 minutes of cooking time, then press "Start."
16. Toss the vegetable after 6 minutes then resume cooking.

17. Once the Instant Pot Duo beeps, remove its lid.
18. Serve.

Nutritional Information per Serving:

- Calories 166
- Total Fat 3.9g
- Saturated Fat 0.5g
- Cholesterol 0mg
- Sodium 51mg

- Total Carbohydrate 30.9g
- Dietary Fiber 5g   18%
- Total Sugars 4.3g
- Protein 3.5g

Sausage Patties

Prep Time: 10 minutes
Cooking Time: 5 minutes
Serving: 4

Ingredients:

- 1 (12 oz.) package sausage patties
- Nonstick cooking spray

Method:

1. Place the sausage patties in the Air Fryer Basket and spray it with cooking oil.
2. Set the Air Fryer Basket in the Instant Pot Duo.
3. Put on the Air Fryer lid and seal it.
4. Hit the "Air fry Button" and select 10 minutes of cooking time, then press "Start."
5. Flip the sausages after 5 minutes then resume cooking.
6. Once the Instant Pot Duo beeps, remove its lid.
7. Serve.

Nutritional Information per Serving:

- Calories 268
- Total Fat 20.4g
- Saturated Fat 5.6g
- Cholesterol 98mg
- Sodium 540mg
- Total Carbohydrate 0g
- Dietary Fiber 0g
- Total Sugars 0g
- Protein 19.8g

Breakfast Tarts

Prep Time: 10 minutes
Cooking Time: 12 minutes
Serving: 4

Ingredients:

- 1 sheet frozen puff pastry
- 4 tablespoons Cheddar cheese, shredded
- 4 tablespoons cooked ham, diced
- 4 eggs
- fresh chives, chopped

Method:

1. Spread the pastry sheet on a flat surface and slice into 4 equal squares.
2. Place 2 pastry squares in the Air Fryer Basket.
3. Set the Air Fryer Basket in the Instant Pot Duo.
4. Put on the Air Fryer lid and seal it.
5. Hit the "Air fry Button" and select 6 minutes of cooking time, then press "Start."
6. Once the Instant Pot Duo beeps, remove its lid.
7. Press the center of each pastry square with the back of a spoon.
8. Add 1 tablespoon cheddar cheese, 1 tablespoon ham, and 1 egg to each of the square groove.
9. Return the basket to the Air fryer.
10. Put on the Air Fryer lid and seal it.
11. Hit the "Air fry Button" and select 6 minutes of cooking time, then press "Start."
12. Once the Instant Pot Duo beeps, remove its lid.
13. Cook the remaining pastry squares in a similar manner.
14. Garnish with chives.
15. Serve.

Nutritional Information per Serving:

- Calories 161
- Total Fat 11.3g
- Saturated Fat 3.7g
- Cholesterol 176mg
- Sodium 241mg
- Total Carbohydrate 5.3g
- Dietary Fiber 0.3g
- Total Sugars 0.5g
- Protein 9.4g

Morning Churros

Prep Time: 10 minutes
Cooking Time: 5 minutes
Serving: 4

Ingredients:

- 1/4 cup butter
- 1/2 cup milk
- 1 pinch salt
- 1/2 cup all-purpose flour
- 2 eggs
- 1/4 cup white sugar
- 1/2 teaspoon ground cinnamon

Method:

1. Melt butter in a 1-quart saucepan and add salt and milk.
2. Stir cook the butter mixture to a boil then stir in flour. Mix it quickly.
3. Remove the butter-flour mixture from the heat and allow the flour mixture to cool down.
4. Stir in egg and mix to get choux pastry and transfer the dough to a pastry bag.
5. Put a star tip on the pastry bag and pine the dough into straight strips in the Air Fryer Basket.
6. Set the Air Fryer Basket in the Instant Pot Duo.
7. Put on the Air Fryer lid and seal it.
8. Hit the "Air fry Button" and select 5 minutes of cooking time, then press "Start."
9. Once the Instant Pot Duo beeps, remove its lid.
10. Mix sugar with cinnamon in a mini bowl and drizzle over the churros.
11. Serve.

Nutritional Information per Serving:

- Calories 253
- Total Fat 14.5g
- Saturated Fat 8.4g
- Cholesterol 115mg
- Sodium 166mg
- Total Carbohydrate 26.3g
- Dietary Fiber 0.6g
- Total Sugars 14.1g
- Protein 5.5g

Zucchini Yogurt Bread

Prep Time: 10 minutes
Cooking Time: 45 minutes
Serving: 6

Ingredients:

- 1 cup walnut halves
- 2 cups all-purpose flour
- 1/2 teaspoon baking powder
- 1/2 teaspoon baking soda
- 1/2 teaspoon salt
- 3/4 cup 2 tablespoons sugar
- 2 large eggs
- 1/2 cup vegetable oil
- 1/2 cup plain Greek yogurt
- 1 cup zucchini, grated

Method:

1. Whisk baking powder, flour, salt, and baking soda in a medium bowl.
2. Stir in eggs, vegetable oil, yogurt, and sugar, then mix well.
3. Add flour mixture and mix well until smooth.
4. Fold in walnuts and zucchini, then spread this batter in a greased baking pan.
5. Place this pan in the Instant Pot Duo.
6. Put on the Air Fryer lid and seal it.
7. Hit the "Bake Button" and select 45 minutes of cooking time, then press "Start."
8. Once the Instant Pot Duo beeps, remove its lid.
9. Slice and serve.

Nutritional Information per Serving:

- Calories 575
- Total Fat 32.8g
- Saturated Fat 5g
- Cholesterol 64mg
- Sodium 333mg
- Total Carbohydrate 60.6g
- Dietary Fiber 2.8g
- Total Sugars 26.4g
- Protein 13.6g

Crumbly Blueberry Muffins

Prep Time: 10 minutes
Cooking Time: 20 minutes
Serving: 6

Ingredients:

Topping

- 1 cup all-purpose flour
- 3 tablespoons brown sugar
- 2 tablespoons granulated sugar
- 1 teaspoon baking powder
- Pinch of salt
- 6 tablespoons butter, melted

Muffins

- 1 3/4 cups all-purpose flour
- 2 1/4 teaspoons baking powder
- 1/2 teaspoon salt
- 1 cup granulated sugar
- 2 large eggs
- 1/2 cup canola oil
- 3/4 cup whole milk
- 1 teaspoon vanilla extract
- 1 1/2 cups blueberries

Method:

1. Layer two muffin trays with paper liners.
2. Whisk flour with brown sugar, granulated sugar, salt, and baking powder in a bowl.
3. Stir in butter and mix to form a crumbly mixture.
4. Now whisk all the Ingredients: for the muffins in a bowl then mix well until smooth.
5. Divide the blueberry batter in the muffin trays and top it with the crumbly mixture.
6. Place a muffin tray in the Instant Pot Duo.
7. Put on the Air Fryer lid and seal it.

8. Hit the "Bake Button" and select 20 minutes of cooking time, then press "Start."
9. Once the Instant Pot Duo beeps, remove its lid.
10. Serve.

Nutritional Information per Serving:

- Calories 587
- Total Fat 32.8g
- Saturated Fat 9.8g
- Cholesterol 96mg
- Sodium 314mg

- Total Carbohydrate 68.9g
- Dietary Fiber 1.9g
- Total Sugars 38.9g
- Protein 7.3g

Gold Potato Blanc Frittata

Prep Time: 10 minutes
Cooking Time: 41 minutes
Serving: 4

Ingredients:

- 2 medium potatoes, unpeeled
- 2 tablespoons unsalted butter
- 2 leeks, sliced
- Salt and black pepper
- 10 large eggs
- 1/3 cup whole milk
- 4 oz. fromage blanc

Method:

1. Take a 2-4-quart saucepan and add water to boil.
2. Place potatoes in this boiling water and cook for 15 minutes then drain.
3. Once the potatoes are cooled, diced them into ½ inch cubes.
4. Sauté leeks with butter in a pan for 4 minutes.
5. Stir in potato cubes and sauté for 3 minutes.
6. Add with some salt and black pepper to adjust seasoning.
7. Beat eggs with milk, salt, and black pepper in a separate bowl.
8. Spread the sautéed veggies in a pan and pour the eggs on top.
9. Place this pan in the Instant Pot Duo.
10. Put on the Air Fryer lid and seal it.
11. Hit the "Bake Button" and select 18 minutes of cooking time, then press "Start."
12. Once the Instant Pot Duo beeps, remove its lid.
13. Serve.

Nutritional Information per Serving:

- Calories 349
- Total Fat 19.1g
- Saturated Fat 8g
- Cholesterol 485mg
- Sodium 293mg
- Total Carbohydrate 24.4g
- Dietary Fiber 2g
- Total Sugars 5.4g
- Protein 21.4g

Saucy Eggs Bake

Prep Time: 10 minutes
Cooking Time: 35 minutes
Serving: 4

Ingredients:

- 1 1/2 pounds plum tomatoes
- 2 garlic cloves, smashed
- 2 tablespoons olive oil
- Salt and ground pepper
- 1 teaspoon oregano, chopped
- 8 large eggs
- 2 tablespoons Parmigiano-Reggiano cheese, grated

Method:

1. Place the tomatoes in the Instant Pot Duo and add garlic, olive oil, salt, and black pepper on top.
2. Put on the Air Fryer lid and seal it.
3. Hit the "Roast Button" and select 20 minutes of cooking time, then press "Start."
4. Once the Instant Pot Duo beeps, remove its lid.
5. Transfer the tomatoes to a blender and puree them with oregano.
6. Take a suitable baking pan and spread the sauce in it.
7. Whisk eggs with salt and black pepper then pour over the sauce.
8. Top it with shredded cheese.
9. Place the egg pan in the Instant Pot Duo.
10. Put on the Air Fryer lid and seal it.
11. Hit the "Bake Button" and select 15 minutes of cooking time, then press "Start."
12. Once the Instant Pot Duo beeps, remove its lid.
13. Serve.

Nutritional Information per Serving:

- Calories 291
- Total Fat 20.3g
- Saturated Fat 6.2g
- Cholesterol 382mg
- Sodium 292mg
- Total Carbohydrate 10.7g
- Dietary Fiber 2.1g
- Total Sugars 7.6g
- Protein 19.3g

Za'atar Eggs Bake

Prep Time: 10 minutes
Cooking Time: 32 minutes
Serving: 4

Ingredients:

- 3 tablespoons olive oil
- 1 medium yellow onion, sliced
- Kosher salt and black pepper
- 2 pints cherry tomatoes
- 2 red bell peppers, chopped
- 1/4 cup 2 teaspoons parsley, chopped
- 2 teaspoons Za'atar
- 4 large eggs
- 1 cup plain yogurt
- 1/2 cup English cucumber, chopped
- 1 tablespoon lemon juice
- 1/2 teaspoon sumac
- 2 teaspoons mint, finely chopped

Method:

1. Take a large skillet and add 2 tablespoon olive oil.
2. Sauté for 5 minutes, then add salt, black pepper, and tomatoes.
3. Cook for 5 minutes and stir in bell peppers. Cook for 10 minutes.
4. Remove the veggie pan from the heat and add half of the parsley and zaatar.
5. Transfer this sauce to a baking pan and make four well into it.
6. Crack an egg into each well and drizzle salt and black pepper on top.
7. Place the egg mixture in the Instant Pot Duo.
8. Put on the Air Fryer lid and seal it.
9. Hit the "Bake Button" and select 12 minutes of cooking time, then press "Start."
10. Once the Instant Pot Duo beeps, remove its lid.
11. Whisk yogurt with lemon juice, sumac, mint, cucumber, salt, and remaining za'atar and parsley in a bowl.
12. Serve the egg bake with this yogurt sauce on top.

Nutritional Information per Serving:

- Calories 203
- Total Fat 15.7g
- Saturated Fat 3.1g
- Cholesterol 186mg
- Sodium 79mg

- Total Carbohydrate 9.6g
- Dietary Fiber 2g
- Total Sugars 5.6g
- Protein 7.8g

Chapter 4: Poultry

Duo Crisp Chicken Wings

Prep Time: 10 minutes
Cooking Time: 18 minutes
Serving: 6

Ingredients:

- 12 chicken wingettes
- 1/2 cup chicken broth
- salt and black pepper to taste
- 1/4 cup melted butter

Method:

1. Set a metal rack in the Instant Pot Duo Crisp and pour broth into it.
2. Place the wingettes on the metal rack then put on its pressure-cooking lid.
3. Hit the "Pressure Button" and select 8 minutes of cooking time, then press "Start."
4. Once the Instant Pot Duo beeps, do a quick release and remove its lid.
5. Transfer the pressure cooked wingettes to a plate.
6. Empty the pot and set an Air Fryer Basket in the Instant Pot Duo
7. Toss the wingettes with butter and seasoning.
8. Spread the seasoned wingettes in the Air Fryer Basket.
9. Put on the Air Fryer lid and hit the Air fryer Button, then set the time to 10 minutes.
10. Remove the lid and serve.
11. Enjoy!

Nutritional Information per Serving:

- Calories 246
- Total Fat 18.9g
- Saturated Fat 7g
- Cholesterol 115mg
- Sodium 149mg
- Total Carbohydrate 0g
- Dietary Fiber 0g
- Total Sugars 0g
- Protein 20.2g

Italian Whole Chicken

Prep Time: 10 minutes
Cooking Time: 35 minutes
Serving: 4

Ingredients:

- 1 whole chicken
- 2 tablespoon or spray of oil of choice
- 1 teaspoon garlic powder
- 1 teaspoon onion powder
- 1 teaspoon paprika
- 1 teaspoon Italian seasoning
- 2 tablespoon Montreal steak seasoning
- 1.5 cup chicken broth

Method:

1. Whisk all the seasoning in a bowl and rub it on the chicken.
2. Set a metal rack in the Instant Pot Duo Crisp and pour broth into it.
3. Place the chicken on the metal rack then put on its pressure-cooking lid.
4. Hit the "Pressure Button" and select 25 minutes of cooking time, then press "Start."
5. Once the Instant Pot Duo beeps, do a natural release and remove its lid.
6. Transfer the pressure-cooked chicken to a plate.
7. Empty the pot and set an Air Fryer Basket in the Instant Pot Duo.
8. Toss the chicken pieces with oil to coat well.
9. Spread the seasoned chicken in the air Fryer Basket.
10. Put on the Air Fryer lid and hit the Air fryer Button, then set the time to 10 minutes.
11. Remove the lid and serve.
12. Enjoy!

Nutritional Information per Serving:

- Calories 163
- Total Fat 10.7g
- Saturated Fat 2g
- Cholesterol 33mg
- Sodium 1439mg
- Total Carbohydrate 1.8g
- Dietary Fiber 0.3g
- Total Sugars 0.8g

- Protein 12.6g

Chicken Pot Pie

Prep Time: 10 minutes
Cooking Time: 17 minutes
Serving: 6

Ingredients:

- 2 tbsp olive oil
- 1-pound chicken breast cubed
- 1 tbsp garlic powder
- 1 tbsp thyme
- 1 tbsp pepper
- 1 cup chicken broth
- 12 oz. bag frozen mixed vegetables
- 4 large potatoes cubed
- 10 oz. Can cream of chicken soup
- 1 cup heavy cream
- 1 pie crust
- 1 egg
- 1 tbsp water

Method:

1. Hit Sauté on the Instant Pot Duo Crispy and add chicken and olive oil.
2. Sauté chicken for 5 minutes then stir in spices.
3. Pour in the broth along with vegetables and cream of chicken soup
4. Put on the pressure-cooking lid and seal it.
5. Hit the "Pressure Button" and select 10 minutes of cooking time, then press "Start."
6. Once the Instant Pot Duo beeps, do a quick release and remove its lid.
7. Remove the lid and stir in cream.
8. Hit sauté and cook for 2 minutes.
9. Enjoy!

Nutritional Information per Serving:

- Calories 568
- Total Fat 31.1g

- Saturated Fat 9.1g
- Cholesterol 95mg
- Sodium 1111mg
- Total Carbohydrate 50.8g

- Dietary Fiber 3.9g
- Total Sugars 18.8g
- Protein 23.4g

Chicken Casserole

Prep Time: 10 Minutes
Cooking Time: 9 minutes
Serving: 6

Ingredients:

- 3 cup chicken, shredded
- 12 oz. bag egg noodles
- 1/2 large onion
- 1/2 cup chopped carrots
- 1/4 cup frozen peas
- 1/4 cup frozen broccoli pieces
- 2 stalks celery chopped
- 5 cup chicken broth
- 1 teaspoon garlic powder
- salt and pepper to taste
- 1 cup cheddar cheese, shredded
- 1 package French's onions
- 1/4 c sour cream
- 1 can cream of chicken and mushroom soup

Method:

1. Add chicken, broth, black pepper, salt, garlic powder, vegetables, and egg noodles to the Instant Pot Duo.
2. Put on the pressure-cooking lid and seal it.
3. Hit the "Pressure Button" and select 4 minutes of cooking time, then press "Start."
4. Once the Instant Pot Duo beeps, do a quick release and remove its lid.
5. Stir in cheese, 1/3 of French's onions, can of soup and sour cream.
6. Mix well and spread the remaining onion top.
7. Put on the Air Fryer lid and seal it.
8. Hit the "Air fryer Button" and select 5 minutes of cooking time, then press "Start."
9. Once the Instant Pot Duo beeps, remove its lid.
10. Serve.

Nutritional Information per Serving:

- Calories 494
- Total Fat 19.1g
- Saturated Fat 9.6g
- Cholesterol 142mg
- Sodium 1233mg

- Total Carbohydrate 29g
- Dietary Fiber 2.6g
- Total Sugars 3.7g
- Protein 48.9g

Ranch Chicken Wings

Prep Time: 10 minutes
Cooking Time: 35 minutes
Serving: 6

Ingredients:

- 12 chicken wings
- 1 tablespoon olive oil
- 1 cup chicken broth
- 1/4 cup butter
- 1/2 cup Red Hot Sauce
- 1/4 teaspoon Worcestershire sauce
- 1 tablespoon white vinegar
- 1/4 teaspoon cayenne pepper
- 1/8 teaspoon garlic powder
- Seasoned salt to taste
- Ranch dressing for dipping
- Celery for garnish

Method:

1. Set the Air Fryer Basket in the Instant Pot Duo and pour the broth in it.
2. Spread the chicken wings in the basket and put on the pressure-cooking lid.
3. Hit the "Pressure Button" and select 10 minutes of cooking time, then press "Start."
4. Meanwhile, prepare the sauce and add butter, vinegar, cayenne pepper, garlic powder, Worcestershire sauce, and hot sauce in a small saucepan.
5. Stir cook this sauce for 5 minutes on medium heat until it thickens.
6. Once the Instant Pot Duo beeps, do a quick release and remove its lid.
7. Remove the wings and empty the Instant Pot Duo.
8. Toss the wings with oil, salt, and black pepper.
9. Set the Air Fryer Basket in the Instant Pot Duo and arrange the wings in it.
10. Put on the Air Fryer lid and seal it.
11. Hit the "Air Fryer Button" and select 20 minutes of cooking time, then press "Start."
12. Once the Instant Pot Duo beeps, remove its lid.

13. Transfer the wings to the sauce and mix well.
14. Serve.

Nutritional Information per Serving:

- Calories 414
- Total Fat 31.6g
- Saturated Fat 11g
- Cholesterol 98mg
- Sodium 568mg

- Total Carbohydrate 11.2g
- Dietary Fiber 0.3g
- Total Sugars 0.2g
- Protein 20.4g

Chicken Mac and Cheese

Prep Time: 10 minutes
Cooking Time: 9 minutes
Serving: 6

Ingredients:

- 2 1/2 cup macaroni
- 2 cup chicken stock
- 1 cup cooked chicken, shredded
- 1 1/4 cup heavy cream
- 8 tablespoon butter
- 2 2/3 cups cheddar cheese, shredded
- 1/3 cup parmesan cheese, shredded
- 1 bag Ritz crackers
- 1/4 teaspoon garlic powder
- Salt and pepper to taste

Method:

1. Add chicken stock, heavy cream, chicken, 4 tablespoon butter, and macaroni to the Instant Pot Duo.
2. Put on the pressure-cooking lid and seal it.
3. Hit the "Pressure Button" and select 4 minutes of cooking time, then press "Start."
4. Crush the crackers and mix them well with 4 tablespoons melted butter.
5. Once the Instant Pot Duo beeps, do a quick release and remove its lid.
6. Put on the Air Fryer lid and seal it.
7. Hit the "Air Fryer Button" and select 5 minutes of cooking time, then press "Start."
8. Once the Instant Pot Duo beeps, remove its lid.
9. Serve.

Nutritional Information per Serving:

- Calories 611
- Total Fat 43.6g
- Saturated Fat 26.8g
- Cholesterol 147mg
- Sodium 739mg
- Total Carbohydrate 29.5g
- Dietary Fiber 1.2g
- Total Sugars 1.7g
- Protein 25.4g

Broccoli Chicken Casserole

Prep Time: 10 minutes
Cooking Time: 22 minutes
Serving: 6

Ingredients:

- 1 1/2 lbs. chicken, cubed
- 2 teaspoon chopped garlic
- 2 tablespoon butter
- 1 1/2 cups chicken broth
- 1 1/2 cups long-grain rice
- 1 (10.75 oz) can cream of chicken soup
- 2 cups broccoli florets
- 1 cup crushed Ritz cracker
- 2 tablespoon melted butter
- 2 cups shredded cheddar cheese

Method:

1. Add 1 cup water to the Instant Pot Dup and place a basket in it.
2. Place the broccoli in the basket evenly.
3. Put on the pressure-cooking lid and seal it.
4. Hit the "Pressure Button" and select 1 minute of cooking time, then press "Start."
5. Once the Instant Pot Duo beeps, do a quick release and remove its lid.
6. Remove the broccoli and empty the Instant Pot Duo.
7. Hit the sauté button then add 2 tablespoon butter.
8. Toss in chicken and stir cook for 5 minutes, then add garlic and sauté for 30 seconds.
9. Stir in rice, chicken broth, and cream of chicken soup.
10. Put on the pressure-cooking lid and seal it.
11. Hit the "Pressure Button" and select 12 minutes of cooking time, then press "Start."
12. Once the Instant Pot Duo beeps, do a quick release and remove its lid.
13. Add cheese and broccoli, then mix well gently.
14. Toss the cracker with 2 tablespoon butter in a bowl and spread over the chicken in the Pot.

15. Put on the Air Fryer lid and seal it.
16. Hit the "Air Fryer Button" and select 4 minutes of cooking time, then press "Start."
17. Once the Instant Pot Duo beeps, remove its lid.
18. Serve.

Nutritional Information per Serving:

- Calories 609
- Total Fat 24.4g
- Saturated Fat 12.6g
- Cholesterol 142mg
- Sodium 924mg

- Total Carbohydrate 45.5g
- Dietary Fiber 1.4g
- Total Sugars 1.6g
- Protein 49.2g

Chicken Tikka Kebab

Prep Time: 10 minutes
Cooking Time: 17 minutes
Serving: 4

Ingredients:

- 1 lb. chicken thighs boneless skinless, cubed
- 1 tablespoon oil
- 1/2 cup red onion, cubed
- 1/2 cup green bell pepper, cubed
- 1/2 cup red bell pepper, cubed
- lime wedges to garnish
- onion rounds to garnish

For marinade:

- 1/2 cup yogurt Greek
- 3/4 tablespoon ginger, grated
- 3/4 tablespoon garlic, minced
- 1 tablespoon lime juice
- 2 teaspoon red chili powder mild
- 1/2 teaspoon ground turmeric
- 1 teaspoon garam masala
- 1 teaspoon coriander powder
- 1/2 tablespoon dried fenugreek leaves
- 1 teaspoon salt

Method:

1. Prepare the marinade by mixing yogurt with all its Ingredients: in a bowl.
2. Fold in chicken, then mix well to coat and refrigerate for 8 hours.
3. Add bell pepper, onions, and oil to the marinade and mix well.
4. Thread the chicken, peppers, and onions on the skewers.
5. Set the Air Fryer Basket in the Instant Pot Duo.
6. Put on the Air Fryer lid and seal it.
7. Hit the "Air Fry Button" and select 10 minutes of cooking time, then press "Start."

8. Once the Instant Pot Duo beeps, and remove its lid.
9. Flip the skewers and continue Air frying for 7 minutes.
10. Serve.

Nutritional Information per Serving:

- Calories 241
- Total Fat 14.2g
- Saturated Fat 3.8g
- Cholesterol 92mg
- Sodium 695mg
- Total Carbohydrate 8.5g
- Dietary Fiber 1.6g
- Total Sugars 3.9g
- Protein 21.8g

Bacon-Wrapped Chicken

Prep Time: 10 minutes
Cooking Time: 24 minutes
Serving: 4

Ingredients:

- 1/4 cup maple syrup
- 1 teaspoon ground black pepper
- 1 teaspoon Dijon mustard
- 1/4 teaspoon garlic powder
- 1/8 teaspoon kosher salt
- 4 (6-oz.) skinless, boneless chicken breasts
- 8 slices bacon

Method:

1. Whisk maple syrup with salt, garlic powder, mustard, and black pepper in a small bowl.
2. Rub the chicken with salt and black pepper and wrap each chicken breast with 2 slices of bacon.
3. Place the wrapped chicken in the Instant Pot baking pan.
4. Brush the wrapped chicken with maple syrup mixture.
5. Put on the Air Fryer lid and seal it.
6. Hit the "Bake Button" and select 20 of cooking time, then press "Start."
7. Once the function is completed, switch the pot to Broil mode and broil for 4 minutes.
8. Serve.

Nutritional Information per Serving:

- Calories 441
- Total Fat 18.3g
- Saturated Fat 5.2g
- Cholesterol 141mg
- Sodium 1081mg
- Total Carbohydrate 14g
- Dietary Fiber 0.1g
- Total Sugars 11.8g
- Protein 53.6g

Creamy Chicken Thighs

Prep Time: 10 minutes
Cooking Time: 25 minutes
Serving: 6

Ingredients:

- 1 tablespoon olive oil
- 6 chicken thighs, bone-in, skin-on
- Salt
- Freshly ground black pepper
- 2 cloves garlic, minced
- 1 tablespoon fresh thyme leaves
- 1 teaspoon crushed red pepper flakes
- 3/4 cup low-sodium chicken broth
- 1/2 cup heavy cream
- 1/2 cup sun-dried tomatoes, chopped
- 1/4 cup Parmesan, grated
- Freshly torn basil, for serving

Method:

1. Hit sauté on the Instant Pot Duo Crisp and add oil to heat.
2. Stir in chicken, salt, and black then sear for 5 minutes per side.
3. Add broth, cream, parmesan, and tomatoes.
4. Put on the Air Fryer lid and seal it.
5. Hit the "Bake Button" and select 20 minutes of cooking time, then press "Start."
6. Once the Instant Pot Duo beeps, remove its lid.
7. Garnish with basil and serve.

Nutritional Information per Serving:

- Calories 454
- Total Fat 37.8g
- Saturated Fat 14.4g
- Cholesterol 169mg
- Sodium 181mg
- Total Carbohydrate 2.8g
- Dietary Fiber 0.7g
- Total Sugars 0.7g
- Protein 26.9g

Chapter 5: Meat

Duo Crisp Ribs

Prep Time: 10 minutes
Cooking Time: 50 minutes
Serving: 2

Ingredients:

- 1 rack of pork ribs

Rub

- 1 1/2 cup broth
- 3 tablespoons Liquid Smoke
- 1 cup Barbecue Sauce

Method:

1. Rub the rib rack with spice rub generously.
2. Pour the liquid into the Instant Pot Duo Crisp.
3. Set an Air Fryer Basket into the Pot and place the rib rack in the basket.
4. Put on the pressure-cooking lid and seal it.
5. Hit the "Pressure Button" and select 30 minutes of cooking time, then press "Start."
6. Once the Instant Pot Duo beeps, do a quick release and remove its lid.
7. Remove the ribs and rub them with barbecue sauce.
8. Empty the pot and place the Air Fryer Basket in it.
9. Set the ribs in the basket, and Air fry them for 20 minutes.
10. Serve.

Nutritional Information per Serving:

- Calories 306
- Total Fat 6.4g
- Saturated Fat 2g
- Cholesterol 32mg
- Sodium 196mg

- Total Carbohydrate 46g
- Dietary Fiber 0.8g
- Total Sugars 33.1g
- Protein 14.7g

Steak a La Mushrooms

Prep Time: 10 minutes
Cooking Time: 18 minutes
Serving: 2

Ingredients:

- 1 lb. Steaks, cubed
- 8 oz. Mushrooms washed and halved
- 2 tablespoons butter, melted
- 1 teaspoon Worcestershire sauce
- 1/2 teaspoon garlic powder, optional
- Salt, to taste
- Fresh cracked black pepper, to taste
- Minced parsley, garnish

Method:

1. Toss the steak cubes with mushrooms, melted butter, garlic powder, salt, black, Worcestershire sauce, black pepper, and salt in a bowl.
2. Place the Air Fryer Basket in the Instant Pot Duo.
3. Spread the steak cubes and mushrooms in the basket.
4. Put on the Air frying lid and seal it.
5. Hit the "Air fryer Button" and select 18 minutes of cooking time, then press "Start."
6. Once the Instant Pot Duo beeps, remove its lid.
7. Garnish with parsley.
8. Serve.

Nutritional Information per Serving:

- Calories 582
- Total Fat 23.2g
- Saturated Fat 11.2g
- Cholesterol 235mg
- Sodium 218mg
- Total Carbohydrate 4.8g
- Dietary Fiber 1.2g
- Total Sugars 2.6g
- Protein 85.7g

Roast Beef

Prep Time: 10 minutes
Cooking Time: 15 minutes
Serving: 4

Ingredients:

- 2 lb. beef roast top
- oil for spraying

Rub

- 1 tbsp kosher salt
- 1 teaspoon black pepper
- 2 teaspoon garlic powder
- 1 teaspoon summer savory

Method:

1. Whisk all the rub Ingredients: in a small bowl.
2. Liberally rub this mixture over the roast.
3. Place an Air Fryer Basket in the Instant Pot Duo and layer it with cooking oil.
4. Set the seasoned roast in the Air Fryer Basket.
5. Put on the Air Fryer lid and seal it.
6. Hit the "Air fry Button" and select 20 minutes of cooking time, then press "Start."
7. Once the Instant Pot Duo beeps, remove its lid.
8. Turn the roast and continue Air fryer for another 15 minutes.
9. Serve warm.

Nutritional Information per Serving:

- Calories 427
- Total Fat 14.2g
- Saturated Fat 5.3g
- Cholesterol 203mg
- Sodium 1894mg
- Total Carbohydrate 1.4g
- Dietary Fiber 0.3g
- Total Sugars 0.3g
- Protein 69.1g

Herbed Vegetable Beef

Prep Time: 10 minutes
Cooking Time: 60 minutes
Serving: 6

Ingredients:

- 3 lbs. beef
- 2 medium onions, sliced
- 2 carrots, chopped
- 2 sticks celery, chopped
- 1 bulb. of garlic, peeled cloves
- 1 bunch mixed fresh herbs (thyme, rosemary, bay, sage)
- olive oil

Method:

1. Add all the vegetables to the Instant Pot Duo Crisp.
2. Top the veggies with the beef roast, olive oil, and herbs.
3. Put on the Air Fryer lid and seal it.
4. Hit the "Bake Button" and select 60 minutes of cooking time, then press "Start."
5. Once the Instant Pot Duo beeps, remove its lid.
6. Serve.

Nutritional Information per Serving:

- Calories 338
- Total Fat 23.5g
- Saturated Fat 8.8g
- Cholesterol 335mg
- Sodium 286mg
- Total Carbohydrate 9.5g
- Dietary Fiber 2.3g
- Total Sugars 4.1g
- Protein 34.8g

Russian Beef Bake

Prep Time: 10 minutes
Cooking Time: 60 minutes
Serving: 6

Ingredients:

- 1 (2 pounds) beef tenderloin
- Salt and ground black pepper to taste
- 2 onions, sliced
- 1 1/2 cups Cheddar cheese, grated
- 1 cup milk
- 3 tablespoons mayonnaise

Method:

1. Slice the beef into thick slices and pound them with a mallet.
2. Place these pounded slices in the Instant Pot Duo's pan.
3. Top these slices with onion, salt, black pepper, cheese, milk, and mayonnaise.
4. Put on the Air Fryer lid and seal it.
5. Hit the "Bake Button" and select 60 minutes of cooking time, then press "Start."
6. Crush the crackers and mix them well with 4 tablespoons melted butter.
7. Once the Instant Pot Duo beeps, remove its lid.
8. Serve.

Nutritional Information per Serving:

- Calories 489
- Total Fat 26.5g
- Saturated Fat 12.1g
- Cholesterol 174mg
- Sodium 338mg
- Total Carbohydrate 7.5g
- Dietary Fiber 0.8g
- Total Sugars 4g
- Protein 52.6g

Beef Pie

Prep Time: 10 minutes
Cooking Time: 65 minutes
Serving: 4

Ingredients:

- 3 tablespoons soy sauce
- 1 tablespoon Worcestershire sauce
- 1/4 cup plain flour
- 1/4 teaspoon salt
- 1/2 teaspoon pepper
- 3 bay leaves
- 3 sprigs thyme
- 2 lbs. lean beef, cubed
- 3 garlic cloves
- 1 carrot, sliced
- 1 onion, sliced
- 6 new potatoes, halved
- 2 celery ribs, sliced
- 1 cup red wine
- 1 cup beef stock
- 2 tablespoons parsley

Method:

1. Whisk seasonings with flour, soy, Worcestershire sauce, thyme, and bay leaves in a pot.
2. Stir cook this sauce for 5 minutes then add carrot, garlic, onion, stock, red wine, and beef.
3. Mix well, then spread this beef mixture into the Instant Pot Duo.
4. Put on the Air Fryer lid and seal it.
5. Hit the "Bake Button" and select 60 minutes of cooking time, then press "Start."
6. Once the Instant Pot Duo beeps, remove its lid.
7. Serve

Nutritional Information per Serving:

- Calories 535
- Total Fat 10.8g
- Saturated Fat 4g
- Cholesterol 149mg
- Sodium 850mg

- Total Carbohydrate 43.7g
- Dietary Fiber 6.4g
- Total Sugars 4.9g
- Protein 56.2g

Pork Chops with Asparagus

Prep Time: 10 minutes
Cooking Time: 25 minutes
Serving: 4

Ingredients:

- 4 pork chops, bone-in
- Salt and Pepper to taste
- 2 tablespoons canola oil
- 1 tablespoon creole seasoning
- 1 1/2 teaspoons minced thyme
- 1 tablespoon garlic, minced
- ½ tablespoon Dijon mustard
- 1 teaspoon Worchester sauce
- 2-3 tablespoons brown sugar
- 2 tablespoons parsley, for garnish
- 1-pound potatoes, cubed
- 1-pound asparagus, chopped

Method:

1. Whisk ½ of the creole seasoning with thyme, garlic, mustard, sugar, oil, and Worcestershire sauce in a bowl.
2. Season the pork chops with this creole mixture and place them in the Air Fryer Basket.
3. Season the potatoes with remaining creole seasoning, oil, and salt.
4. Place these potatoes around the pork chops in the Air Fryer Basket.
5. Set the Air basket in the Instant Pot Duo.
6. Put on the Air Fryer lid and seal it.
7. Hit the "Bake Button" and select 22 minutes of cooking time, then press "Start."
8. Once the Instant Pot Duo beeps, switch it to Broil mode and cook for 3 minutes.
9. Garnish with parsley and enjoy.

Nutritional Information per Serving:

- Calories 467
- Total Fat 27.1g
- Saturated Fat 8g
- Cholesterol 69mg
- Sodium 992mg
- Total Carbohydrate 34.8g
- Dietary Fiber 5.8g
- Total Sugars 11.6g
- Protein 21.1g

Pork Chops with Potatoes

Prep Time: 10 minutes
Cooking Time: 17 minutes
Serving: 4

Ingredients:

Rub

- 1 teaspoon Worcestershire Sauce
- 2 tablespoon ketchup
- 1 tablespoon soy sauce
- 2 tablespoon brown sugar
- 1 tablespoon olive oil
- 1 clove garlic, minced
- 2 teaspoon apple cider vinegar

Chops

- 4 pork chops
- 1 tablespoon olive oil
- Salt & pepper

Method:

1. Mix all the marinade Ingredients: in a bowl and rub it liberally over the pork chops.
2. Cover these pork chops and refrigerate for 1 hour.
3. Transfer the pork chops in the Air Fryer Basket and set it inside the Instant Pot Duo.
4. Put on the Air Fryer lid and seal it.
5. Hit the "Bake Button" and select 15 minutes of cooking time, then press "Start."
6. Once the Instant Pot Duo beeps, remove its lid and flip the chops.
7. Switch the Instant Pot Duo to the Broil mode for 2 minutes and put on Air Fryer lid.
8. Serve warm.

Nutritional Information per Serving:

- Calories 315
- Total Fat 23.4g

- Saturated Fat 8g
- Cholesterol 69mg
- Sodium 380mg
- Total Carbohydrate 7.1g
- Dietary Fiber 0.1g
- Total Sugars 6.4g
- Protein 18.4g

Basic Pork Chops

Prep Time: 10 minutes
Cooking Time: 15 minutes
Serving: 4

Ingredients:

- 4 pork chops, bone-in
- 1 tablespoon olive oil
- 1 teaspoon kosher salt
- 1/2 teaspoon black pepper

Method:

1. Liberally season the pork chops with olive oil, salt, and black pepper.
2. Place the pork chops in the Air Fryer Basket and spray them with cooking spray.
3. Set the Air Fryer Basket in the Instant Pot Duo.
4. Put on the Air Fryer lid and seal it.
5. Hit the "Air fry Button" and select 15 minutes of cooking time, then press "Start."
6. Once the Instant Pot Duo beeps, remove its lid.
7. Serve and enjoy.

Nutritional Information per Serving:

- Calories 287
- Total Fat 23.4g
- Saturated Fat 8g
- Cholesterol 69mg
- Sodium 637mg
- Total Carbohydrate 0.2g
- Dietary Fiber 0.1g
- Total Sugars 0g
- Protein 18g

Breaded Pork Chops

Prep Time: 10 minutes
Cooking Time: 18 minutes
Serving: 4

Ingredients:

- 4 boneless, center-cut pork chops, 1-inch thick
- 1 teaspoon Cajun seasoning
- 1 1/2 cups garlic-flavored croutons
- 2 eggs
- cooking spray

Method:

1. Grind croutons in a food processor until it forms crumbs.
2. Season the pork chops with Cajun seasoning liberally.
3. Beat eggs in a shallow tray then dip the pork chops in the egg.
4. Coat the dipped chops in the crouton crumbs.
5. Place the breaded pork chops in the Air Fryer Basket.
6. Set the Air Fryer Basket and spray the chops with cooking oil.
7. Put on the Air Fryer lid and seal it.
8. Hit the "Air fry Button" and select 18 minutes of cooking time, then press "Start."
9. Once the Instant Pot Duo beeps, remove its lid.
10. Serve.

Nutritional Information per Serving:

- Calories 301
- Total Fat 12.4g
- Saturated Fat 2.6g
- Cholesterol 160mg
- Sodium 256mg
- Total Carbohydrate 12.2g
- Dietary Fiber 0g
- Total Sugars 0.2g
- Protein 32.2g

Chapter 6: Fish and Seafood

Fish in Garlic-Chili Sauce

Prep Time: 10 minutes
Cooking Time: 15 minutes
Serving: 2

Ingredients:

Sauce

- 1/4 cup oyster sauce
- 1/4 cup soy sauce
- 8 to 10 cloves garlic, minced
- 1 tablespoon fish sauce
- 2 tablespoons brown sugar
- 1/4 teaspoon black pepper
- 1 tablespoon lime juice
- 3 red chilies, chopped

For the Fish

- 2 whole red snappers
- 1 handful fresh coriander
- 1 handful fresh basil
- 4 tablespoon oil

Method:

1. Prepare the sauce by mixing all its Ingredients: in a bowl.
2. Make a foil packet for each fish fillet and place a fillet in the pocket.
3. Place the fish pockets in the Instant Pot Duo and top them with prepared sauce.
4. Put on the Air Fryer lid and seal it.
5. Hit the "Air fry Button" and select 10 minutes of cooking time, then press "Start."
6. Once the Instant Pot Duo beeps, switch the Instant Pot to Broil mode.
7. Broil the fish for 5 minutes in the pot.
8. Serve.

Nutritional Information per Serving:

- Calories 265
- Total Fat 1.4g
- Saturated Fat 0.3g
- Cholesterol 0mg
- Sodium 2952mg
- Total Carbohydrate 22.4g
- Dietary Fiber 0.7g
- Total Sugars 10g
- Protein 3.5g

Halibut with Mushroom Sauce

Prep Time: 10 minutes
Cooking Time: 26 minutes
Serving: 4

Ingredients:

- 4 halibut fillets
- 2 tablespoons butter
- Salt to taste
- Black pepper to taste

Sauce

- 3 tablespoons butter
- 4 to 6 oz. mushrooms, sliced
- 4 to 6 green onions, trimmed, sliced
- 3 tablespoons flour
- 1/2 cup chicken broth
- 1 cup milk
- 1 tablespoon sherry
- 1/2 teaspoon seasoned salt
- 1/4 teaspoon garlic-seasoned pepper

Method:

1. Mix melted butter with black pepper and salt in a small bowl.
2. Brush the halibut fillets with butter mixture then place them in the Instant Pot Duo.
3. Put on the Air Fryer lid and seal it.
4. Hit the "Bake Button" at 350 degrees F and select 25 minutes of cooking time, then press "Start."
5. Meanwhile, prepare the mushroom sauce and add butter to a saucepan.
6. Melt it then add mushrooms then sauté until golden brown.
7. Stir in green onion, then cook for 1 minute and stir in flour.
8. Slowly add milk, chicken broth, seasonings, and sherry, then stir cook until it thickens.
9. Once the Instant Pot Duo beeps, remove its lid.

10. Transfer the halibut to the serving plate.
11. Top the halibut with mushroom sauce.
12. Serve.

Nutritional Information per Serving:

- Calories 451
- Total Fat 14.1g
- Saturated Fat 5.4g
- Cholesterol 113mg
- Sodium 515mg

- Total Carbohydrate 9.7g
- Dietary Fiber 0.8g
- Total Sugars 3.7g
- Protein 64.9g

Flounder with Lemon Butter

Prep Time: 10 minutes
Cooking Time: 15 minutes
Serving: 4

Ingredients:

- 1 1/2 pounds flounder fillets, diced
- 1 teaspoon salt
- 1/8 teaspoon black pepper
- 4 tablespoons butter, melted
- 2 tablespoons lemon juice
- 2 teaspoons onion, minced
- 1 teaspoon paprika

Method:

1. Spread the flounder pieces in a baking dish.
2. Drizzle salt and black pepper on top of the flounder.
3. Whisk melted butter with onion and lemon juice.
4. Pour this lemon-onion mixture over the fish along with paprika.
5. Place this pan in the Instant Pot Duo.
6. Put on the Air Fryer lid and seal it.
7. Hit the "bake Button" and select 15 minutes of cooking time, then press "Start."
8. Once the Instant Pot Duo beeps, remove its lid.
9. Serve.

Nutritional Information per Serving:

- Calories 305
- Total Fat 14.3g
- Saturated Fat 8g
- Cholesterol 146mg
- Sodium 844mg
- Total Carbohydrate 0.7g
- Dietary Fiber 0.3g
- Total Sugars 0.3g
- Protein 41.4g

Herbed Sea Bass

Prep Time: 10 minutes
Cooking Time: 10 minutes
Serving: 4

Ingredients:

- 4 sea bass
- 1 1/2 to 2 bunches of parsley, finely chopped
- 5 cloves of garlic, sliced
- 2 tablespoons of lemon juice
- 2 tablespoons of olive oil
- Sea salt
- 1 tablespoon oregano
- 24 slices of tomato
- Olive oil
- 1 cup white wine
- 3 cups of water

Method:

1. Whisk lemon juice, parsley, garlic, oregano, salt, and olive oil in a bowl.
2. Add this parsley mixture inside the fish.
3. Pour water and wine into the Instant Pot Duo.
4. Place the stuffed fish in the wine mixture and top it with tomato slices.
5. Put on the Air Fryer lid and seal it.
6. Hit the "Bake Button" and select 10 minutes of cooking time, then press "Start."
7. Once the Instant Pot Duo beeps, remove its lid.
8. Serve.

Nutritional Information per Serving:

- Calories 198
- Total Fat 7.9g
- Saturated Fat 1.1g
- Cholesterol 0mg
- Sodium 9mg
- Total Carbohydrate 5.9g
- Dietary Fiber 1.8g
- Total Sugars 2.7g
- Protein 27.3g

White Fish with Cilantro Sauce

Prep Time: 10 minutes
Cooking Time: 30 minutes
Serving: 4

Ingredients:

- 1 large bunch of cilantro, chopped
- 1 small onion, chopped
- 3 cloves of fresh garlic, peeled and chopped
- 3 tablespoons butter
- 2 cups sour cream
- 2 teaspoons salt
- 4 tablespoons lime juice
- 2 1/2 pounds white fish fillets

Method:

1. Add butter to a suitably sized skillet to melt over medium heat.
2. Stir in garlic and onion, then sauté for 5 minutes, then transfer to a blender.
3. Add cream, cilantro, salt, and lime juice, then puree this sauce until smooth.
4. Place the fish fillets in the Instant Pot Duo basket.
5. Put on the Air Fryer lid and seal it.
6. Hit the "Bake Button" and select 25 minutes of cooking time, then press "Start."
7. Once the Instant Pot Duo beeps, do a quick release and remove its lid.
8. Serve.

Nutritional Information per Serving:

- Calories 462
- Total Fat 33.8g
- Saturated Fat 20.7g
- Cholesterol 135mg
- Sodium 1375mg
- Total Carbohydrate 11g
- Dietary Fiber 0.6g
- Total Sugars 1.7g
- Protein 29.9g

Sole with Mint and Ginger

Prep Time: 10 minutes
Cooking Time: 15 minutes
Serving: 4

Ingredients:

- 2 pounds sole fillets
- 1 bunch mint
- 1 2-inch piece ginger, peeled and chopped
- 1 tablespoon vegetable or canola oil
- 1/2 teaspoon salt
- 1/4 teaspoon freshly ground black pepper

Method:

1. Add mint, salt, black pepper, ginger, and oil to a blender and blend until smooth.
2. Stir in 2 teaspoon water if the sauce is too thick then mix well.
3. Rub the fish with the mint sauce to coat it liberally.
4. Place the coated fish in the Instant Pot Duo.
5. Put on the Air Fryer lid and seal it.
6. Hit the "Air fry Button" and select 15 minutes of cooking time, then press "Start."
7. Once the Instant Pot Duo beeps, remove its lid.
8. Serve warm.

Nutritional Information per Serving:

- Calories 302
- Total Fat 7.6g
- Saturated Fat 0.3g
- Cholesterol 147mg
- Sodium 559mg
- Total Carbohydrate 1g
- Dietary Fiber 0.3g
- Total Sugars 0g
- Protein 50.9g

Bacon-Wrapped Shrimp

Prep Time: 10 minutes
Cooking Time: 10 minutes
Serving: 6

Ingredients:

- 1-pound shrimp
- 1 package bacon
- 1/2 teaspoon cayenne pepper
- 1/2 teaspoon ground cumin
- 1/2 teaspoon onion powder
- 1/2 teaspoon lemon zest
- 1 teaspoon garlic powder
- 1 tablespoon Worcestershire sauce
- 1 tablespoon lemon juice

Method:

1. Whisk Worcestershire sauce with cayenne pepper, onion powder, cumin, lemon zest, and garlic powder in a large bowl.
2. Toss in shrimp and mix well to coat then cover them to refrigerate for 1 hour.
3. Cut the bacon in half and wrap each half around each shrimp.
4. Place the wrapped shrimp in the Air Fryer Basket and set it in the Instant Pot Duo.
5. Put on the Air Fryer lid and seal it.
6. Hit the "Air fry Button" and select 10 minutes of cooking time, then press "Start."
7. Once the Instant Pot Duo beeps, remove its lid.
8. Serve.

Nutritional Information per Serving:

- Calories 114
- Total Fat 2.7g
- Saturated Fat 0.9g
- Cholesterol 163mg
- Sodium 286mg
- Total Carbohydrate 2.4g
- Dietary Fiber 0.1g
- Total Sugars 0.8g
- Protein 18.6g

Horseradish Crusted Salmon

Prep Time: 10 minutes
Cooking Time: 5 minutes
Serving: 2

Ingredients:

- 2 pieces of salmon fillet
- 1 teaspoon salt
- 1 teaspoon black pepper
- 1 tablespoon horseradish
- 2 tablespoons olive oil
- 1/4 cup bread crumbs

Method:

1. Whisk bread crumbs with salt, olive oil, horseradish and black pepper in a bowl.
2. Coat the salmon with this crumbly mixture liberally.
3. Place the breaded salmon in the Air Fryer Basket and set it inside the Instant Pot Duo.
4. Put on the Air Fryer lid and seal it.
5. Hit the "Air fry Button" and select 5 minutes of cooking time, then press "Start."
6. Once the Instant Pot Duo beeps, remove its lid.
7. Serve.

Nutritional Information per Serving:

- Calories 415
- Total Fat 25.8g
- Saturated Fat 3.8g
- Cholesterol 78mg
- Sodium 1364mg
- Total Carbohydrate 11.3g
- Dietary Fiber 1.1g
- Total Sugars 1.5g
- Protein 36.5g

Pesto Shrimp Kebobs

Prep Time: 10 minutes
Cooking Time: 5 minutes
Serving: 12

Ingredients:

- 1-pound shrimp
- 16 oz. basil pesto

Method:

1. Toss the shrimp with pesto and coat them well.
2. Thread these pesto shrimp on the skewers.
3. Place the skewers in the Air Fryer Basket and set it in the Instant Pot Duo.
4. Put on the Air Fryer lid and seal it.
5. Hit the "Air fry Button" and select 5 minutes of cooking time, then press "Start."
6. Once the Instant Pot Duo beeps, remove its lid.
7. Serve.

Nutritional Information per Serving:

- Calories 92
- Total Fat 1.3g
- Saturated Fat 0.3g
- Cholesterol 147mg
- Sodium 172mg
- Total Carbohydrate 2g
- Dietary Fiber 1.2g
- Total Sugars 0.2g
- Protein 18.2g

Shrimp on the Sticks

Prep Time: 10 minutes
Cooking Time: 5 minutes
Serving: 6

Ingredients:

- 1-pound shrimp, peeled and deveined
- 1/4 cup butter, melted
- 1 tablespoon Old Bay Seasoning
- 1 tablespoon brown sugar
- 1 teaspoon garlic powder
- 1 teaspoon onion powder
- 1/2 teaspoon ground cumin
- 1/2 teaspoon ground red pepper
- 1 teaspoon minced garlic

Method:

1. Thread the shrimp on the skewers and keep them aside.
2. Mix melted butter with cumin, red pepper, garlic, onion powder, garlic powder, brown sugar, and bay seasoning in a bowl.
3. Brush this butter sauce over the shrimp skewers. Liberally.
4. Place these skewers in the Air Fryer Basket and set them in the Instant Pot Duo.
5. Put on the Air Fryer lid and seal it.
6. Hit the "Air fry Button" and select 5 minutes of cooking time, then press "Start."
7. Once the Instant Pot Duo beeps, remove its lid.
8. Serve.

Nutritional Information per Serving:

- Calories 168
- Total Fat 9g
- Saturated Fat 5.3g
- Cholesterol 180mg
- Sodium 560mg
- Total Carbohydrate 3.6g
- Dietary Fiber 0.1g
- Total Sugars 1.7g
- Protein 17.5g

Chapter 7: Vegetables

Broccoli and Cauliflower Medley

Prep Time: 10 minutes
Cooking Time: 10 minutes
Serving: 2

Ingredients:

- 1/2 lb. broccoli fresh
- 1/2 lb. cauliflower fresh
- 1 tablespoon olive oil
- 1/4 teaspoon black pepper
- 1/4 teaspoon salt
- 1/4 teaspoon garlic salt
- 1/3 cup water

Method:

1. Toss the vegetable with seasonings and olive oil in a bowl.
2. Pour 1/3 cup water into the Instant Pot duo base.
3. Place the Air fry basket inside and spread the vegetables in it.
4. Put on the Air Fryer lid and seal it.
5. Hit the "Roast Button" and select 10 minutes of cooking time, then press "Start."
6. Once the Instant Pot Duo beeps, remove its lid.
7. Serve.

Nutritional Information per Serving:

- Calories 90
- Total Fat 7g
- Saturated Fat 1g
- Cholesterol 0mg
- Sodium 324mg
- Total Carbohydrate 7.4g
- Dietary Fiber 3.1g
- Total Sugars 2.8g
- Protein 3.1g

Roasted Squash Mix

Prep Time: 10 minutes
Cooking Time: 40 minutes
Serving: 2

Ingredients:

- 3 potatoes, cubed
- 1 red onion, quartered
- 1 butternut squash, cubed
- 1 sweet potato, peeled and cubed
- 1 tablespoon fresh thyme, chopped
- 2 tablespoons fresh rosemary, chopped
- 2 red bell peppers, seeded and diced
- 1/4 cup olive oil
- 2 tablespoons balsamic vinegar
- Salt and freshly ground black pepper

Method:

1. Whisk rosemary with thyme, vinegar, olive oil, black pepper, and salt in a bowl.
2. Toss in onion, bell peppers, squash, potatoes, and sweet potato.
3. Add the vegetables to the Instant Pot Duo.
4. Put on the Air Fryer lid and seal it.
5. Hit the "Roast Button" and select 40 minutes of cooking time, then press "Start."
6. Toss the roasting vegetables every 10 minutes.
7. Once the Instant Pot Duo beeps, remove its lid.
8. Serve.

Nutritional Information per Serving:

- Calories 570
- Total Fat 26.7g
- Saturated Fat 4g
- Cholesterol 0mg
- Sodium 58mg
- Total Carbohydrate 82.8g
- Dietary Fiber 11.5g
- Total Sugars 15.4g
- Protein 9.2g

Zucchini Satay

Prep Time: 10 minutes
Cooking Time: 10 minutes
Serving: 2

Ingredients:

- 2 zucchinis, sliced
- 2 yellow squash, sliced
- 1 container mushrooms, halved
- 1/2 cup olive oil
- 1/2 onion sliced
- 3/4 teaspoon Italian seasoning
- 1/2 teaspoon garlic salt
- 1/4 teaspoon seasoned salt

Method:

1. Toss zucchini, squash, onion, and mushrooms in a large bowl.
2. Whisk olive oil, with Italian seasoning, salt, and garlic salt in a small bowl.
3. Pour this olive oil mixture into the vegetables then toss well.
4. Spread the seasoned veggies in the Air Fryer Basket.
5. Set the Air Fryer Basket in the Instant Pot Duo.
6. Put on the Air Fryer lid and seal it.
7. Hit the "Air fry Button" and select 10 minutes of cooking time, then press "Start."
8. Once the Instant Pot Duo beeps, remove its lid.
9. Serve.

Nutritional Information per Serving:

- Calories 492
- Total Fat 51.4g
- Saturated Fat 7.4g
- Cholesterol 1mg
- Sodium 22mg
- Total Carbohydrate 11.8g
- Dietary Fiber 4.2g
- Total Sugars 5.5g
- Protein 4.7g

Cauliflower Cheese Pasta

Prep Time: 10 minutes
Cooking Time: 27 minutes
Serving: 4

Ingredients:

- 9 oz. shell pasta, cooked and drained
- 3.5 oz. unsalted butter
- 2 bay leaves
- 1 onion, chopped
- 3 garlic cloves, crushed
- 1/2 bunch sage, chopped
- 1 tbsp plain flour
- 3 3/4 cups cream
- 7 oz. smoked cheese, coarsely grated
- 1 1/4 cups parmesan, grated
- 1 large cauliflower, blanched, cut into wedges
- 1/4 teaspoon nutmeg, grated

Method:

1. Place a frypan over medium-high heat and add butter.
2. Melt it and add garlic, onion, and bay leave then sauté for 5 minutes.
3. Discard the bay leaves, then stir in flour and sage. Stir cook for 2 minutes.
4. Slowly add cream, cheese, pasta, and parmesan, then add crumbled cauliflower.
5. Stir in nutmeg and seasoning, then transfer to the Instant Pot Duo.
6. Put on the Air Fryer lid and seal it.
7. Hit the "Bake Button" and select 20 minutes of cooking time, then press "Start."
8. Once the Instant Pot Duo beeps, remove its lid.
9. Serve.

Nutritional Information per Serving:

- Calories 427
- Total Fat 23.8g
- Saturated Fat 14.4g
- Cholesterol 106mg
- Sodium 263mg
- Total Carbohydrate 43.1g
- Dietary Fiber 2.5g
- Total Sugars 2.9g
- Protein 12.1g

Pumpkin Baked Gnocchi

Prep Time: 10 minutes
Cooking Time: 46 minutes
Serving: 6

Ingredients:

- 26 oz. potato gnocchi, cooked
- 1/3 cup olive oil
- 16 sage leaves
- 26 oz. pumpkin, cut into slices
- 2 egg yolks
- 2 ½ cup cream
- 1/2 teaspoon finely grated nutmeg
- 3/4 cup coarsely grated mozzarella
- 3.5 oz. blue cheese, crumbled
- Roasted chopped hazelnuts, to serve

Method:

1. Mix pumpkin with 1 tablespoon oil in a bowl.
2. Stir in egg yolks, cream, gnocchi, half of the sage, half of the blue cheese, nutmeg, cream, and mozzarella.
3. Spread this mixture in the Instant Pot Duo insert.
4. Top the casserole with remaining cheese.
5. Put on the Air Fryer lid and seal it.
6. Hit the "Bake Button" and select 45 minutes of cooking time, then press "Start."
7. Once the Instant Pot Duo beeps, remove its lid.
8. Heat ¼ cup in a frying pan and add sage. Sauté for 1 minute.
9. Transfer the fried sage to a plate lined with a paper towel.
10. Add this fried sage, and nuts to the casserole.
11. Garnish with sage oil.
12. Serve.

Nutritional Information per Serving:

- Calories 537
- Total Fat 30.8g
- Saturated Fat 13g
- Cholesterol 122mg
- Sodium 560mg
- Total Carbohydrate 50.1g
- Dietary Fiber 0.8g
- Total Sugars 0.9g
- Protein 17.8g

Pumpkin Lasagna

Prep Time: 10 minutes
Cooking Time: 60 minutes
Serving: 6

Ingredients:

- 28 oz. pumpkin, cut into slices
- 1 bunch sage, chopped
- 1/2 cup ghee, melted
- 1 leek, thinly sliced
- 4 garlic cloves, finely grated
- 3.5 oz. kale and cavolo Nero leaves shredded
- 270g semi-dried tomatoes, drained, chopped
- 17 Oz. quark
- 2 eggs, lightly beaten

Method:

1. Mix pumpkin slices with sage leaves, 2 teaspoon salt, 2 tablespoon ghee in a bowl.
2. Toss leek separately with 2 tablespoon ghee, garlic, and ½ teaspoon salt in another bowl.
3. Mix kale with 1 teaspoon salt, tomato, and cavolo Nero in a bowl.
4. Now beat eggs with quark and sage in a bowl.
5. Take a baking pan that can fit into the Instant Pot Duo.
6. Add 1/3 of the leek mixture at the base of the baking pan.
7. Top this mixture with a layer of pumpkin slices.
8. Add 1/3 of quark mixture on top then add 1/3 of kale mixture over it.
9. Top it with pumpkin slices and continue repeating the layer while ending at the pumpkin slice layer on top.
10. Place the baking pan in the Instant Pot duo.
11. Put on the Air Fryer lid and seal it.
12. Hit the "Bake Button" and select 60 minutes of cooking time, then press "Start."
13. Once the Instant Pot Duo beeps, remove its lid.
14. Serve.

Nutritional Information per Serving:

- Calories 491
- Total Fat 29.9g
- Saturated Fat 16.9g
- Cholesterol 147mg
- Sodium 1462mg

- Total Carbohydrate 52.1g
- Dietary Fiber 9.7g
- Total Sugars 28g
- Protein 14.8g

Haloumi Baked Rusti

Prep Time: 10 minutes
Cooking Time: 35 minutes
Serving: 4

Ingredients:

- Olive oil, to brush
- 7 oz. sweet potato, coarsely grated
- 10 oz. potatoes, coarsely grated
- 10 oz. carrots, coarsely grated
- 9 oz. halloumi, coarsely grated
- 1/2 onion, coarsely grated
- 2 tbsp thyme leaves
- 2 eggs
- 1/3 cup plain flour
- 1/2 cup sour cream, to serve

Fennel Salad

- 2 celery stalks, thinly sliced
- 1 fennel, thinly sliced
- 1/2 cup olives, chopped
- Juice of 1 lemon
- 1 lemon quarter, chopped
- 1 teaspoon toasted coriander seeds, ground

Method:

1. Toss sweet potato, carrot, potato, onion, halloumi, thyme, flour, and eggs in a bowl.
2. Spread this mixture in the Instant Pot Duo insert.
3. Put on the Air Fryer lid and seal it.
4. Hit the "Bake Button" and select 35 minutes of cooking time, then press "Start."
5. Once the Instant Pot Duo beeps, remove its lid.
6. Prepare the salad by mixing its Ingredients: in a salad bowl.
7. Serve the sweet potato rosti with the prepared salad.

Nutritional Information per Serving:

- Calories 462
- Total Fat 21.1g
- Saturated Fat 12.8g
- Cholesterol 124mg
- Sodium 1064mg

- Total Carbohydrate 43.9g
- Dietary Fiber 5.9g
- Total Sugars 8.9g
- Protein 23g

Celeriac Potato Gratin

Prep Time: 10 minutes
Cooking Time: 63 minutes
Serving: 6

Ingredients:

- 2 cups cream
- 1 teaspoon caraway seeds, toasted
- 1 garlic clove, crushed
- 1 teaspoon fennel seeds, toasted
- 2 bay leaves
- 1/4 teaspoon ground cloves
- Zest of 1/2 a lemon
- 2 teaspoon melted butter
- 1kg potatoes, peeled
- 1 cup celeriac, peeled and minced
- 6 slices prosciutto, torn
- 3/4 cup fresh ricotta
- ¼ cup fontina cheese, grated

Method:

1. Add cream, garlic, caraway seeds, cloves, bay leaves, fennel, zest, and cloves to a saucepan.
2. Stir cook this mixture for 3 minutes then remove from the heat.
3. Thinly slices potato by passing through the mandolin and spread the potatoes in the insert of Instant Pot Duo.
4. Top the potato with celeriac, prepared white sauce, prosciutto, and ricotta.
5. Put on the Air Fryer lid and seal it.
6. Hit the "Bake Button" and select 60 minutes of cooking time, then press "Start."
7. Once the Instant Pot Duo beeps, remove its lid.
8. Serve.

Nutritional Information per Serving:

- Calories 399
- Total Fat 20.3g

- Saturated Fat 10.9g
- Cholesterol 99mg
- Sodium 1484mg
- Total Carbohydrate 23.6g
- Dietary Fiber 3.8g
- Total Sugars 4.8g
- Protein 31.3g

Eggplant Pine Nut Roast

Prep Time: 10 minutes
Cooking Time: 66 minutes
Serving: 6

Ingredients:

- 6 Japanese eggplants
- 2/3 cup olive oil
- 1 onion, finely chopped
- 4 garlic cloves, crushed
- 1 1/2 tbsp sundried tomato pesto
- 1 teaspoon smoked paprika
- 14 oz. can cherry tomatoes
- 1 teaspoon zaatar, plus extra to serve
- 2/3 cup vegetable stock
- 1/2 bunch mint, chopped
- 2 tbsp toasted pine nuts, roughly crushed
- 1/4 cup Greek yogurt
- Juice of 1 lemon

Method:

1. Add eggplants to the Air Fryer Basket and pour 2 tablespoon oil over them.
2. Set the Air Fryer Basket in the Instant Pot Duo.
3. Put on the Air Fryer lid and seal it.
4. Hit the "Bake Button" and select 30 minutes of cooking time, then press "Start."
5. Once the Instant Pot Duo beeps, remove its lid.
6. Meanwhile, prepare the sauce by sautéing onion with remaining oil in a pan.
7. After 4 minutes, add garlic to sauté for 2 minutes.
8. Add tomato, stock, zaatar, paprika and tomato pesto.
9. Cook this sauce for 10 minutes until it thickens.
10. Pour this sauce over the eggplant and continue baking it for another 20 minutes.
11. Mix yogurt with lemon juice, mint, and pine nuts.
12. Serve the baked eggplants with yogurt.

Nutritional Information per Serving:

- Calories 413
- Total Fat 25g
- Saturated Fat 3.7g
- Cholesterol 0mg
- Sodium 85mg

- Total Carbohydrate 45g
- Dietary Fiber 22.1g
- Total Sugars 27.2g
- Protein 9.2g

Roasted Veggie Casserole

Prep Time: 10 minutes
Cooking Time: 50 minutes
Serving: 6

Ingredients:

- ½ head cauliflower, cut into chunks
- 1 sweet potato, peeled and cubed
- 2 red bell peppers, cubed
- 1 yellow onion, sliced
- 3 tablespoons olive oil
- 1 teaspoon ground cumin
- Salt
- Freshly ground black pepper
- 2 ¼ cups red salsa
- ½ cup chopped fresh cilantro
- 9 corn tortillas cut in half
- 1 can (15 oz.) black beans, drained
- 2 big handfuls (about 2 oz.) baby spinach leaves
- 2 cups Monterey Jack cheese, shredded

Method:

1. Toss the vegetables with olive oil, salt, black pepper, and cumin in a large bowl.
2. Add these vegetables to the Air Fryer Basket and set it inside the Instant Pot Duo.
3. Put on the Air Fryer lid and seal it.
4. Hit the "Bake Button" and select 30 minutes of cooking time, then press "Start."
5. Once the Instant Pot Duo beeps, remove its lid.
6. Transfer the veggies to a baking pan and top it with salsa, tortilla, beans, spinach, and cheese.
7. Place this pan in the Instant Pot Duo.
8. Put on the Air Fryer lid and seal it.
9. Hit the "Bake Button" and select 20 minutes of cooking time, then press "Start."
10. Once the Instant Pot Duo beeps, remove its lid.
11. Serve.

Nutritional Information per Serving:

- Calories 390
- Total Fat 20.5g
- Saturated Fat 8.4g
- Cholesterol 34mg
- Sodium 686mg

- Total Carbohydrate 38.7g
- Dietary Fiber 7.4g
- Total Sugars 9.6g
- Protein 15.8g

Chapter 8: Snacks

Paneer Cheese Balls

Prep Time: 10 minutes
Cooking Time: 15 minutes
Serving: 6

Ingredients:

- 1 cup paneer, crumbled
- 1 cup cheese, grated
- 1 potato, boiled and mashed
- 1 onion, chopped finely
- 1 green chili, chopped finely
- 1 teaspoon red chili flakes
- salt to taste
- 4 tbsp coriander leaves, chopped finely
- ½ cup all-purpose flour
- ¾ cup of water
- Breadcrumbs as needed

Method:

1. Mix flour with water in a bowl and spread the breadcrumbs in a tray.
2. Add the rest of the Ingredients: to make the paneer mixture.
3. Make golf ball-sized balls out of this mixture.
4. Dip each ball in the flour liquid then coat with the breadcrumbs.
5. Place the cheese balls in the Instant Pot Duo and spray it with cooking spray.
6. Put on the Air Fryer lid and seal it.
7. Hit the "Air fry Button" and select 15 minutes of cooking time, then press "Start."
8. Once the Instant Pot Duo beeps, remove its lid.
9. Serve.

Nutritional Information per Serving:

- Calories 227
- Total Fat 10.6g
- Saturated Fat 5.7g
- Cholesterol 25mg
- Sodium 207mg
- Total Carbohydrate 23.4g
- Dietary Fiber 1.7g
- Total Sugars 3.6g
- Protein 9.9g

Russet Potato Hay

Prep Time: 10 minutes
Cooking Time: 15 minutes
Serving: 4

Ingredients:

- 2 russet potatoes
- 1 tablespoon olive oil
- Salt and black pepper to taste

Method:

1. Pass the potatoes through a spiralizer to get potato spirals.
2. Soak these potato spirals in a bowl filled with water for about 20 minutes.
3. Drain and rinse the soaked potatoes then pat them dry.
4. Toss the potato spirals with salt, black pepper, and oil in a bowl.
5. Spread the seasoned potato spirals in the Air Fryer Basket.
6. Set this Air Fryer Basket in the Instant Pot duo.
7. Put on the Air Fryer lid and seal it.
8. Hit the "Air fry Button" and select 15 minutes of cooking time, then press "Start."
9. Toss the potato spiral when halfway cooked then resume cooking.
10. Once the Instant Pot Duo beeps, remove its lid.
11. Serve.

Nutritional Information per Serving:

- Calories 104
- Total Fat 3.6g
- Saturated Fat 0.3g
- Cholesterol 0mg 0%
- Sodium 6mg
- Total Carbohydrate 16.7g
- Dietary Fiber 2.6g
- Total Sugars 1.2g
- Protein 1.8g

Onion Rings

Prep Time: 10 minutes
Cooking Time: 10 minutes
Serving: 4

Ingredients:

- 3/4 cup flour
- 1 large yellow onion, sliced and rings separated
- ¼ tsp garlic powder
- ¼ tsp paprika
- 1 cup almond milk
- 1 large egg
- 1/2 cup cornstarch
- 1 ½ teaspoons of baking powder
- 1 teaspoon salt
- 1 cup bread crumbs
- cooking spray

Method:

1. Whisk flour with baking powder, salt, and cornstarch in a bowl.
2. Coat the onion rings with this dry flour mixture and keep them aside.
3. Beat egg with milk in a bowl and dip the rings in this mixture.
4. Place the coated rings in the Air Fryer Basket and set it inside the Instant Pot Duo.
5. Spray the onion rings with cooking oil. Put on the Air Fryer lid and seal it.
6. Hit the "Air fry Button" and select 10 minutes of cooking time, then press "Start."
7. Flip the rings when cooked halfway through.
8. Once the Instant Pot Duo beeps, remove its lid.
9. Serve.

Nutritional Information per Serving:

- Calories 319
- Total Fat 4.2g
- Saturated Fat 1.5g
- Cholesterol 46mg
- Sodium 829mg
- Total Carbohydrate 59.9g
- Dietary Fiber 2.9g
- Total Sugars 6.2g
- Protein 9.9g

Breaded Avocado Fries

Prep Time: 10 minutes
Cooking Time: 7 minutes
Serving: 4

Ingredients:

- 1/4 cup all-purpose flour
- 1/2 teaspoon ground black pepper
- 1/4 teaspoon salt
- 1 egg
- 1 teaspoon water
- 1 ripe avocado, peeled, pitted and sliced
- 1/2 cup panko bread crumbs
- cooking spray

Method:

1. Whisk flour with salt and black pepper in one bowl.
2. Beat egg with water in another and spread the crumbs in a shallow tray.
3. First coat the avocado slices with the flour mixture then dip them into the egg.
4. Drop off the excess and coat the avocado with panko crumbs liberally.
5. Place all the coated slices in the Air Fryer Basket and spray them with cooking oil.
6. Set the Air Fryer Basket inside the Instant Pot Duo.
7. Put on the Air Fryer lid and seal it.
8. Hit the "Air fry Button" and select 7 minutes of cooking time, then press "Start."
9. Flip the fries after 4 minutes of cooking and resume cooking.
10. Once the Instant Pot Duo beeps, remove its lid.
11. Serve fresh.

Nutritional Information per Serving:

- Calories 201
- Total Fat 11.7g
- Saturated Fat 2.6g
- Cholesterol 41mg
- Sodium 265mg
- Total Carbohydrate 20.3g
- Dietary Fiber 4.3g
- Total Sugars 1.2g
- Protein 5g

Buffalo Chicken Strips

Prep Time: 10 minutes
Cooking Time: 8 minutes
Serving: 4

Ingredients:

- 1/2 cup Greek yogurt
- 1/4 cup egg
- 1 ½ tablespoon hot sauce
- 1 cup panko bread crumbs
- 1 tablespoon sweet paprika
- 1 tablespoon garlic pepper seasoning
- 1 tablespoon cayenne pepper
- 1-pound chicken breasts, cut into strips

Method:

1. Mix Greek yogurt with hot sauce and egg in a bowl.
2. Whisk bread crumbs with garlic powder, cayenne pepper, and paprika in another bowl.
3. First, dip the chicken strips in the yogurt sauce then coat them with the crumb's mixture.
4. Place the coated strips in the Air Fryer Basket and spray them with cooking oil.
5. Set the Air Fryer Basket inside the Instant Pot Duo.
6. Put on the Air Fryer lid and seal it.
7. Hit the "Air fry Button" and select 16 minutes of cooking time, then press "Start."
8. Flip the chicken strips after 8 minutes of cooking then resume Air fearing.
9. Once the Instant Pot Duo beeps, remove its lid.
10. Serve.

Nutritional Information per Serving:

- Calories 368
- Total Fat 11.8g
- Saturated Fat 3.2g
- Cholesterol 157mg
- Sodium 413mg
- Total Carbohydrate 23.5g
- Dietary Fiber 2.5g
- Total Sugars 3.1g
- Protein 40.4g

Sweet Potato Chips

Prep Time: 10 minutes
Cooking Time: 13 minutes
Serving: 2

Ingredients:

- 1 teaspoon avocado oil
- 1 medium sweet potato, peeled and sliced
- 1/2 teaspoon Creole seasoning

Method:

1. Toss the sweet potato with avocado oil and creole seasoning in a bowl.
2. Spread the potato slices in the Air Fryer Basket and spray them with oil.
3. Set the Air Fryer Basket in the Instant Pot Duo.
4. Put on the Air Fryer lid and seal it.
5. Hit the "Air fry Button" and select 13 minutes of cooking time, then press "Start."
6. Toss the potato slices after 7 minutes of cooking and resume air frying.
7. Once the Instant Pot Duo beeps, remove its lid.
8. Serve fresh.

Nutritional Information per Serving:

- Calories 55
- Total Fat 0.4g
- Saturated Fat 0.1g
- Cholesterol 0mg
- Sodium 291mg
- Total Carbohydrate 11.9g
- Dietary Fiber 2g
- Total Sugars 3.7g
- Protein 1.2g

Sweet Potato Tots

Prep Time: 10 minutes
Cooking Time: 16 minutes
Serving: 4

Ingredients:

- 2 sweet potatoes, peeled
- 1/2 teaspoon Cajun seasoning
- olive oil cooking spray
- sea salt to taste

Method:

1. Add sweet potatoes to boiling water in a pot and cook for 15 minutes until soft.
2. Drain the boiled sweet potatoes and allow them to cool down.
3. Grate the potatoes into a bowl and stir in Cajun seasoning and salt.
4. Mix well and make small tater tots out of this mixture.
5. Place these tater tots in the Air Fryer Basket and spray them with cooking oil.
6. Set the Air Fryer Basket in the Instant Pot Duo.
7. Put on the Air Fryer lid and seal it.
8. Hit the "Air fry Button" and select 16 minutes of cooking time, then press "Start."
9. After 8 minutes, flip all the tots and spray them again with cooking oil then resume cooking.
10. Once the Instant Pot Duo beeps, remove its lid.
11. Serve fresh.

Nutritional Information per Serving:

- Calories 89
- Total Fat 0.1g
- Saturated Fat 0g
- Cholesterol 0mg
- Sodium 72mg
- Total Carbohydrate 20.9g
- Dietary Fiber 3.1g
- Total Sugars 0.4g
- Protein 1.2g

Corn Nuts

Prep Time: 10 minutes
Cooking Time: 20 minutes
Serving: 6

Ingredients:

- 14 oz. giant white corn
- 3 tablespoons vegetable oil
- 1 1/2 teaspoons salt

Method:

1. Soak white corn in a bowl filled with water and leave it for 8 hours.
2. Drain the soaked corns and spread them in the Air Fryer Basket.
3. Leave to dry for 20 minutes after patting them dry with a paper towel.
4. Add oil and salt on top of the corns and toss them well.
5. Set the Air Fryer Basket in the Instant Pot.
6. Put on the Air Fryer lid and seal it.
7. Hit the "Air fry Button" and select 20 minutes of cooking time, then press "Start."
8. Shake the corns after every 5 minutes of cooking, then resume the function.
9. Once the Instant Pot Duo beeps, remove its lid.
10. Serve.

Nutritional Information per Serving:

- Calories 128
- Total Fat 7.8g
- Saturated Fat 1.3g
- Cholesterol 0mg
- Sodium 581mg
- Total Carbohydrate 14.3g
- Dietary Fiber 1.4g
- Total Sugars 2.1g
- Protein 2.1g

Tempura Vegetables

Prep Time: 10 minutes
Cooking Time: 10 minutes
Serving: 4

Ingredients:

- 1/2 cup all-purpose flour
- 1/2 teaspoon salt, divided, or more to taste
- 1/2 teaspoon ground black pepper
- 2 eggs
- 2 tablespoons water
- 1 cup panko bread crumbs
- 2 teaspoons vegetable oil
- 1/2 cup whole green beans
- 1/2 cup asparagus spears
- 1/2 cup red onion rings
- 1/2 cup sweet pepper rings
- 1/2 cup avocado wedges
- 1/2 cup zucchini slices

Method:

1. Whisk flour with black pepper and salt in a shallow dish.
2. Beat eggs with water in a bowl and mix panko with oil in another tray.
3. Coat all the veggies with flour mixture first, then dip them in egg and finally in the panko mixture to a coat.
4. Shake off the excess and keep the coated veggies in separate plates.
5. Set half of the coated vegetables in a single layer in the Air Fryer Basket.
6. Place the basket in the Instant Pot Duo and spray them with cooking oil.
7. Put on the Air Fryer lid and seal it.
8. Hit the "Air fry Button" and select 10 minutes of cooking time, then press "Start."
9. Once the Instant Pot Duo beeps, remove its lid.
10. Transfer the fried veggies to the serving plates and cooking the remaining half using the same steps.
11. Serve.

Nutritional Information per Serving:

- Calories 275
- Total Fat 9.7g
- Saturated Fat 2.2g
- Cholesterol 82mg
- Sodium 395mg

- Total Carbohydrate 37.7g
- Dietary Fiber 3.9g
- Total Sugars 4.5g
- Protein 9.5g

Shrimp a La Bang Sauce

Prep Time: 10 minutes
Cooking Time: 12 minutes
Serving: 6

Ingredients:

- 1/2 cup mayonnaise
- 1/4 cup sweet chili sauce
- 1 tablespoon sriracha sauce
- 1/4 cup all-purpose flour
- 1 cup panko bread crumbs
- 1-pound raw shrimp, peeled and deveined
- 1 head loose-leaf lettuce
- 2 green onions, chopped, or to taste

Method:

1. Whisk mayonnaise with sriracha, chili sauce in a bowl until smooth.
2. Spread flour in one plate and panko in the other.
3. Place flour on a plate. Place panko on a separate plate.
4. First coat the shrimp with the flour, then dip in mayonnaise mixture and finally coat with the panko.
5. Arrange the shrimp in the Air Fryer Basket in a single layer. (do not overcrowd)
6. Set the Air Fryer Basket in the Instant Pot Duo.
7. Put on the Air Fryer lid and seal it.
8. Hit the "Air fry Button" and select 12 minutes of cooking time, then press "Start."
9. Once the Instant Pot Duo beeps, remove its lid.
10. Air fry the remaining shrimp in the same way.
11. Garnish with lettuce and green onion.
12. Serve.

Nutritional Information per Serving:

- Calories 285
- Total Fat 8.9g
- Saturated Fat 1.6g
- Cholesterol 164mg
- Sodium 542mg
- Total Carbohydrate 28.8g
- Dietary Fiber 1.4g
- Total Sugars 7g
- Protein 20.7g

Chapter 9: Desserts

Cake Bites with Fudge Sauce

Prep Time: 10 minutes
Cooking Time: 16 minutes
Serving: 12

Ingredients:

- 2/3 cup heavy cream
- 1/2 cup Light Corn Syrup
- 1/3 cup brown sugar
- 1/4 cup cocoa powder
- 1/2 teaspoon salt
- 7 oz. baking chocolate
- 2 tablespoon butter
- 1 teaspoon vanilla extract
- 5 oz. Irish Cream
- 1 Pound Cake

Method:

1. Mix corn syrup, cream, sugar, salt, cocoa powder, and 4 oz. Chocolate in a saucepan and stir cook for 5 minutes.
2. Remove it from the heat then stir in Irish cream, vanilla extract, butter, and remaining chocolate.
3. Mix well and allow this sauce to thicken.
4. Meanwhile, slice the pound cake into 1 ½ inch cubes using a sharp knife.
5. Place these cake cubes in the Air Fryer Basket and spray them with cooking oil.
6. Set the Air Fryer Basket in the Instant Pot Duo.
7. Put on the Air Fryer lid and seal it.
8. Hit the "Air fry Button" and select 11 minutes of cooking time, then press "Start."
9. Toss the cake cubes after 6 minutes then resume cooking.
10. Once the Instant Pot Duo beeps, remove its lid.
11. Serve the cubes with chocolate sauce.
12. Enjoy.

Nutritional Information per Serving:

- Calories 462
- Total Fat 20.4g
- Saturated Fat 10.6g
- Cholesterol 39mg
- Sodium 258mg

- Total Carbohydrate 57.5g
- Dietary Fiber 1.2g
- Total Sugars 24.3g
- Protein 4.3g

Apple Chips with Almond Dip

Prep Time: 10 minutes
Cooking Time: 12 minutes
Serving: 4

Ingredients:

- 1 (8-oz.) apple
- 1 teaspoon ground cinnamon
- 2 teaspoons canola oil
- Cooking spray
- 1/4 cup Greek yogurt
- 1 tablespoon almond butter
- 1 teaspoon honey

Method:

1. Pass the apple through a mandolin to get thin slices.
2. Add these slices to a bowl and add oil and cinnamon them toss well.
3. Place the slices in the Air Fryer Basket in a single layer.
4. Set the Air Fryer Basket in the Instant Pot Duo.
5. Put on the Air Fryer lid and seal it.
6. Hit the "Air fry Button" and select 12 minutes of cooking time, then press "Start."
7. Flip the slices after every 4 minutes then resume cooking.
8. Once the Instant Pot Duo beeps, remove its lid.
9. Air fry the remaining slices in the same manner.
10. Whisk yogurt with honey and almond butter in a bowl.
11. Serve the apple crisp with yogurt on top.

Nutritional Information per Serving:

- Calories 292
- Total Fat 5.5g
- Saturated Fat 0.4g
- Cholesterol 0mg
- Sodium 10mg
- Total Carbohydrate 65.5g
- Dietary Fiber 11.5g
- Total Sugars 48.9g
- Protein 2.4g

Blueberry Cheesecake

Prep Time: 10 minutes
Cooking Time: 15 minutes
Serving: 6

Ingredients:

- 6 digestives
- 2 oz. butter, melted
- 5 cups soft cheese
- 1 ½ cups caster sugar
- 4 large eggs
- 3.5 oz. fresh blueberries
- 2 tablespoon Greek yogurt
- 1 tablespoon vanilla essence
- 5 tablespoon icing sugar

Method:

1. Take a 6-inch springform pan and dust it with flour.
2. Crush digestive biscuits in a food processor and mix with melted butter.
3. Spread the biscuit crumb in the pan and press it evenly.
4. Beat cream cheese with sugar in an electric mixer until fluffy.
5. Stir in eggs, vanilla essence, and yogurt then mix well.
6. Fold in chopped berries and mix gently with the filling.
7. Spread the blueberry-cream filling in the crust evenly.
8. Place the prepared pan in the Air Fryer Basket.
9. Set the Air Fryer Basket in the Instant Pot Duo.
10. Put on the Air Fryer lid and seal it.
11. Hit the "Air fry Button" and select 15 minutes of cooking time, then press "Start."
12. Once the Instant Pot Duo beeps, remove its lid.
13. Allow the cake to cool down then transfer to the refrigerator for 4 hours.
14. Garnish with icing sugar.
15. Slice and serve.

Nutritional Information per Serving:

- Calories 686
- Total Fat 27.1g

- Saturated Fat 9.4g
- Cholesterol 142mg
- Sodium 305mg
- Total Carbohydrate 91.9g
- Dietary Fiber 2.4g
- Total Sugars 64.7g
- Protein 20.8g

Oats Sandwich Biscuits

Prep Time: 10 minutes
Cooking Time: 18 minutes
Serving: 6

Ingredients:

- 1 ½ cups plain flour
- 3.5 oz. butter
- 3 oz. white sugar
- ½ small egg beaten
- ¼ cup desiccated coconut
- ½ cup gluten-free oats
- 1/3 oz. white chocolate
- 1 teaspoon vanilla essence

Filling:

- 3.5 oz. icing sugar
- 2 oz. butter
- 1/2 teaspoon lemon juice
- 1 teaspoon vanilla essence

Method:

1. Whisk butter with sugar in an electric mixer until fluffy.
2. Stir in egg, vanilla essence, coconut, and chocolate then mix well.
3. Slow add flour and continue mixing until it forms a cookie dough.
4. Make medium-sized biscuits out of it then roll them in the oats to coat.
5. Place the cookies in the Air Fryer Basket. Cook the cookies in batches to avoid overcrowding.
6. Set the Air Fryer Basket in the Instant Pot Duo.
7. Put on the Air Fryer lid and seal it.
8. Hit the "Air fry Button" and select 18 minutes of cooking time, then press "Start."
9. Flip the cookies after 9 minutes then resume cooking.
10. Once the Instant Pot Duo beeps, remove its lid.
11. Air fry the remaining cookies in the same manner.
12. Meanwhile, beat butter with icing sugar into a creamy mixture.

13. Stir in vanilla and lemon juice, then mix well.
14. Spread a tablespoon of this filling in between two cookies and make a sandwich out of them.
15. Use the entire filling to make more cookie sandwiches.
16. Serve.

Nutritional Information per Serving:

- Calories 389
- Total Fat 16.4g
- Saturated Fat 10.1g
- Cholesterol 37mg
- Sodium 103mg
- Total Carbohydrate 57.4g
- Dietary Fiber 2.4g
- Total Sugars 31.1g
- Protein 4.6g

Chocolate Smarties Cookies

Prep Time: 10 minutes
Cooking Time: 15 minutes
Serving: 6

Ingredients:

- 3.5 oz. butter
- 3.5 oz. caster sugar
- 8 oz. self-rising flour
- 1 teaspoon vanilla essence
- 5 tablespoon milk
- 3 tablespoon cocoa powder
- 2 oz. nestle smarties

Method:

1. Whisk cocoa powder with caster sugar and self-rising flour in a bowl.
2. Stir in butter and mix well to form a crumbly mixture.
3. Stir in milk and vanilla essence, then mix well to form a smooth dough.
4. Add the smarties and knead the dough well.
5. Roll this cookie dough into a 1-inch thick layer.
6. Use a cookies cutter to cut maximum cookies out of it.
7. Roll the remaining dough again to carve out more cookies.
8. Place half of the cookies in the Air Fryer Basket.
9. Set the Air Fryer Basket in the Instant Pot Duo.
10. Put on the Air Fryer lid and seal it.
11. Hit the "Bake Button" and select 10 minutes of cooking time, then press "Start."
12. Flip the cookies after 5 minutes then resume cooking.
13. Once the Instant Pot Duo beeps, remove its lid.
14. Bake the remaining cookies in a similar way.
15. Enjoy.

Nutritional Information per Serving:

- Calories 372
- Total Fat 16g
- Saturated Fat 9.8g
- Cholesterol 38mg
- Sodium 108mg
- Total Carbohydrate 53.3g
- Dietary Fiber 2.1g
- Total Sugars 23.3g
- Protein 5.3g

Strawberry Cupcakes

Prep Time: 10 minutes
Cooking Time: 8 minutes
Serving: 6

Ingredients:

- 3.5 oz. butter
- 3.5 oz. caster sugar
- 2 medium eggs
- 3.5 oz. self-rising flour
- ½ teaspoon vanilla essence

Topping

- 2 oz. butter
- 3.5 oz. icing sugar
- ½ teaspoon pink food coloring
- 1 tablespoon whipped cream
- 1 oz. fresh strawberries blended

Method:

1. Beat butter with sugar in a mixer until fluffy.
2. Stir in eggs, and vanilla then beat well.
3. Slowly add flour while mixing the batter.
4. Divide this mixture into a mini muffin tray, greased with cooking spray.
5. Place the muffin tray in the Instant Pot Duo.
6. Put on the Air Fryer lid and seal it.
7. Hit the "Bake Button" and select 8 minutes of cooking time, then press "Start."
8. Once the Instant Pot Duo beeps, remove its lid.
9. Meanwhile, beat the cream with the rest of the Ingredients: in a beater until fluffy.
10. Add this topping to a piping bag and pipe the topping on top of the baked cupcakes.
11. Serve.

Nutritional Information per Serving:

- Calories 337
- Total Fat 15.9g

- Saturated Fat 9.5g
- Cholesterol 93mg
- Sodium 118mg
- Total Carbohydrate 46.3g
- Dietary Fiber 0.5g
- Total Sugars 33.2g
- Protein 3.8g

Crumbly Fruit Cakes

Prep Time: 10 minutes
Cooking Time: 15 minutes
Serving: 4

Ingredients:

- 4 oz. plain flour
- 2 oz. butter
- 1 oz. caster sugar
- 1 oz. gluten-free oats
- 1 oz. brown sugar
- 4 plums, cored and chopped
- 1 small apple, cored and chopped
- 1 small pear, cored and chopped
- 1 small peach, cored and chopped
- handful blueberries, quartered
- 1 tablespoon honey

Method:

1. Add all the fruits to a bowl and divide them into 4 ramekins.
2. Drizzle honey and brown sugar over the fruits in each ramekin.
3. Whisk flour with caster sugar and butter in a mixing bowl to get a crumbly mixture.
4. Divide this crumble into the ramekins then place these ramekins in the Instant Pot Duo.
5. Put on the Air Fryer lid and seal it.
6. Hit the "Air fry Button" and select 10 minutes of cooking time, then press "Start."
7. Once the Instant Pot Duo beeps, switch it Broil mode and broil for 5 minutes.
8. Remove the lid and serve.

Nutritional Information per Serving:

- Calories 388
- Total Fat 11.4g
- Saturated Fat 6.5g
- Cholesterol 27mg
- Sodium 75mg
- Total Carbohydrate 70.9g
- Dietary Fiber 6.2g
- Total Sugars 39.4g
- Protein 5.1g

Strawberry Jam Tart

Prep Time: 10 minutes
Cooking Time: 10 minutes
Serving: 6

Ingredients:

- 8 oz. plain flour
- 3.5 oz. butter
- 1 oz. caster sugar
- 1 cup of strawberry jam
- water

Method:

1. Mix flour with butter and sugar in a mixing bowl to get a crumbly mixture.
2. Slowly stir in water and mix well to make a pastry dough.
3. Layer a pie pan with the pastry dough evenly.
4. Add the strawberry jam on top of the pastry dough.
5. Place the pie pan in the Instant Pot Duo.
6. Put on the Air Fryer lid and seal it.
7. Hit the "Air fry Button" and select 10 minutes of cooking time, then press "Start."
8. Once the Instant Pot Duo beeps, remove its lid.
9. Slice and serve.

Nutritional Information per Serving:

- Calories 474
- Total Fat 13.9g
- Saturated Fat 8.6g
- Cholesterol 36mg
- Sodium 97mg
- Total Carbohydrate 82.4g
- Dietary Fiber 1g
- Total Sugars 4.3g
- Protein 4g

Shortbread Fingers

Prep Time: 10 minutes
Cooking Time: 12 minutes
Serving: 12

Ingredients:

- 6 oz. Butter
- 3 oz. Caster Sugar
- 9 oz. Plain Flour

Method:

1. Mix flour with sugar and butter in a bowl.
2. Knead this shortbread dough well until smooth.
3. Make 4- finger shapes out of this dough and place them in the Air Fryer Basket.
4. Set the Air Fryer Basket in the Instant Pot Duo.
5. Put on the Air Fryer lid and seal it.
6. Hit the "Air fry Button" and select 12 minutes of cooking time, then press "Start."
7. Flip the shortbread cookies after 6 minutes then resume cooking.
8. Once the Instant Pot Duo beeps, remove its lid.
9. Serve.

Nutritional Information per Serving:

- Calories 204
- Total Fat 12g
- Saturated Fat 7.5g
- Cholesterol 31mg
- Sodium 84mg
- Total Carbohydrate 22.2g
- Dietary Fiber 0.6g
- Total Sugars 6.3g
- Protein 2.3g

Fruit Crumble Pie

Prep Time: 10 minutes
Cooking Time: 15 minutes
Serving: 6

Ingredients:

- 3 oz. plain flour
- 1 oz. butter
- 1 oz. caster sugar
- 1 medium red apple, peeled and diced
- 4 medium plums, diced
- 1 oz. frozen berries, diced
- 1 teaspoon cinnamon

Method:

1. Toss all the fruits into the insert of the Instant Pot Duo.
2. Whisk flour with sugar and butter to make a crumble.
3. Spread this crumble over the fruits evenly.
4. Put on the Air Fryer lid and seal it.
5. Hit the "Bake Button" and select 15 minutes of cooking time, then press "Start."
6. Once the Instant Pot Duo beeps, remove its lid.
7. Slice and serve.

Nutritional Information per Serving:

- Calories 149
- Total Fat 4.8g
- Saturated Fat 2.8g
- Cholesterol 12mg
- Sodium 32mg
- Total Carbohydrate 26.3g
- Dietary Fiber 2.3g
- Total Sugars 14.2g
- Protein 1.9g

Chapter 10: 21 Days Meal Plan

Week 01

Day 1

Breakfast: Sweet Potato Hash

Lunch: Roast Beef

Snack: Sweet Potato Tots

Dinner: Fish in Garlic-Chili Sauce

Dessert: Cake Bites with Fudge Sauce

Day 2

Breakfast: Vegetable Hash

Lunch: Steak A La Mushrooms

Snack: Sweet Potato Chips

Dinner: Halibut with Mushroom Sauce

Dessert: Apple Chips with Almond Dip

Day 3

Breakfast: Sausage Patties

Lunch: Duo Crisp Ribs

Snack: Buffalo Chicken Strips

Dinner: Flounder with Lemon Butter

Dessert: Blueberry Cheesecake

Day 4

Breakfast: Breakfast Tarts

Lunch: Pizza Pasta

Snack: Onion Rings

Dinner: Herbed Sea Bass

Dessert: Oats Sandwich Biscuits

Day 5

Breakfast: Morning Churros

Lunch: Creamy Chicken Thighs

Snack: Shrimp a la Bang Sauce

Dinner: White Fish with Cilantro Sauce

Dessert: Chocolate Smarties Cookies

Day 6

Breakfast: Zucchini Yogurt Bread

Lunch: Bacon-Wrapped Chicken

Snack: Tempura Vegetables

Dinner: Sole with Mint and Ginger

Dessert: Strawberry Cupcakes

Day 7

Breakfast: Crumbly Blueberry Muffins

Lunch: Chicken Tikka Kebab

Snack: Corn Nuts

Dinner: Bacon Wrapped Shrimp

Dessert: Strawberry Jam Tart

Week 02

Day 1

Breakfast: Gold Potato Blanc Frittata

Lunch: Broccoli Chicken Casserole

Snack: Sweet Potato Tots

Dinner: Horseradish Crusted Salmon

Dessert: Shortbread Fingers

Day 2

Breakfast: Saucy Eggs Bake

Lunch: Chicken Mac and Cheese

Snack: Sweet Potato Chips

Dinner: Pesto Shrimp Kebobs

Dessert: Fruit Crumble Pie

Day 3

Breakfast: Za'atar Eggs Bake

Lunch: Ranch Chicken Wings

Snack: Buffalo Chicken Strips

Dinner: Broccoli and Cauliflower Medley

Dessert: Cake Bites with Fudge Sauce

Day 4

Breakfast: Sweet Potato Hash

Lunch: Chicken Casserole

Snack: Breaded Avocado Fries

Dinner: Roasted Squash Mix

Dessert: Apple Chips with Almond Dip

Day 5

Breakfast: Vegetable Hash

Lunch: Chicken Pot Pie

Snack: Onion Rings

Dinner: Zucchini Satay

Dessert: Blueberry Cheesecake

Day 6

Breakfast: Sausage Patties

Lunch: Italian Whole Chicken

Snack: Russet Potato Hay

Dinner: Cauliflower Cheese Pasta

Dessert: Oats Sandwich Biscuits

Day 7

Breakfast: Breakfast Tarts

Lunch: Duo Crisp Chicken Wings

Snack: Paneer Cheese Balls

Dinner: Pumpkin Baked Gnocchi

Dessert: Chocolate Smarties Cookies

Week 03

Day 1

Breakfast: Sweet Potato Hash

Lunch: Roast Beef

Snack: Sweet Potato Tots

Dinner: Fish in Garlic-Chili Sauce

Dessert: Cake Bites with Fudge Sauce

Day 2

Breakfast: Vegetable Hash

Lunch: Steak A La Mushrooms

Snack: Sweet Potato Chips

Dinner: Halibut with Mushroom Sauce

Dessert: Apple Chips with Almond Dip

Day 3

Breakfast: Sausage Patties

Lunch: Duo Crisp Ribs

Snack: Buffalo Chicken Strips

Dinner: Flounder with Lemon Butter

Dessert: Blueberry Cheesecake

Day 4

Breakfast: Breakfast Tarts

Lunch: Pizza Pasta

Snack: Onion Rings

Dinner: Herbed Sea Bass

Dessert: Oats Sandwich Biscuits

Day 5

Breakfast: Morning Churros

Lunch: Creamy Chicken Thighs

Snack: Shrimp a la Bang Sauce

Dinner: White Fish with Cilantro Sauce

Dessert: Chocolate Smarties Cookies

Day 6

Breakfast: Zucchini Yogurt Bread

Lunch: Bacon-Wrapped Chicken

Snack: Tempura Vegetables

Dinner: Sole with Mint and Ginger

Dessert: Strawberry Cupcakes

Day 7

Breakfast: Crumbly Blueberry Muffins

Lunch: Chicken Tikka Kebab

Snack: Corn Nuts

Dinner: Bacon Wrapped Shrimp

Dessert: Strawberry Jam Tart

Conclusion

With those many recipes and a comprehensive guideline about the Instant Pot Duo Crisp, now you know how to put to its best use and enjoy a range of flavorsome crispy meals in no time. this ten in one multipurpose kitchen miracle has brought much-wanted peace and comfort to the lives of the homemakers who can now cook a healthy and delicious meal for their family, in no time. The different segment of this book provides a step by step method to cook a variety of meals ranging from breakfast, poultry, meat, vegetarian, snacks and much more. Get this latest hit of the Instant Pot series and bring convenience to your kitchen floor now!